AFGHANISTAN REMEMBERS

Gendered Narrations of Violence and Culinary Practices

Although an extensive academic literature exists on the subject of violence, little attention has been given to the ways in which violence becomes entrenched and normalized in the inner recesses of everyday life. In *Afghanistan Remembers*, Parin Dossa examines how violence is remembered by Afghan women through memories and food practices in their homeland and its diaspora. Her work reveals how the suffering and trauma of violence has been rendered socially invisible following decades of life in a war-zone.

Dossa argues that it is necessary to acknowledge the impact of violence on the familial lives of Afghan women along with their attempts at rebuilding their lives under difficult circumstances. Informed by Dossa's own story of family migration and loss, *Afghanistan Remembers* is a poignant ethnographic account of the trauma of war in Afghanistan and its diaspora that calls on the reader to recognize and bear witness to the impact of deeper forms of violence.

PARIN DOSSA is a professor of anthropology in the Department of Sociology and Anthropology at Simon Fraser University.

PARIN DOSSA

Afghanistan Remembers

Gendered Narrations of Violence and Culinary Practices

UNIVERSITY OF TORONTO PRESS
Toronto Buffalo London

© University of Toronto Press 2014
Toronto Buffalo London
www.utppublishing.com
Printed in the U.S.A.

Reprinted 2015

ISBN 978-1-4426-4724-4 (cloth)
ISBN 978-1-4426-1537-3 (paper)

Library and Archives Canada Cataloguing in Publication

Dossa, Parin, 1945–, author
Afghanistan remembers : gendered narrations of violence
and culinary practices / Parin Dossa.

Includes bibliographical references and index.
ISBN 978-1-4426-4724-4 (bound).   ISBN 978-1-4426-1537-3 (pbk.)

1. Women – Afghanistan – Social conditions.   2. Women – Afghanistan – Social
life and customs.   3. Women and war – Afghanistan.   4. Afghan War, 2001– –
Women – Social conditions.   5. Afghan War, 2001– – Personal narratives,
Afghan.   6. Collective memory – Afghanistan.   7. Afghan Canadian women –
Social conditions.   8. Afghan Canadian women – Social life and customs.
9. Collective memory – Canada.   I. Title.

HQ1735.6.D68 2014   305.48'891593   C2014-901136-9

University of Toronto Press acknowledges the financial assistance to its
publishing program of the Canada Council for the Arts and the
Ontario Arts Council, an agency of the Government of Ontario.

 Canada Council   Conseil des Arts
for the Arts   du Canada

ONTARIO ARTS COUNCIL
CONSEIL DES ARTS DE L'ONTARIO
an Ontario government agency
un organisme du gouvernement de l'Ontario

University of Toronto Press acknowledges the financial support of the
Government of Canada through the Canada Book Fund for its
publishing activities.

بسم الله الرحمن الرحيم

Bismi Llahi Al Rahmani Al Raheem
In the Name of Allah, the Compassionate, the Merciful

Contents

Acknowledgments

I owe my greatest debt of thanks to all the women who brought this study to fruition. Their contributions ranged from life-history interviews, storytelling, conversations, and invitations to their homes and festivals. My debt to their generosity and kindness is immense. I have attempted to safeguard their anonymity by changing personal names, identity markers, and certain place names. I hope that I have done justice to the trust they showed me throughout the course of my research in Afghanistan and Canada.

I acknowledge the research assistants that I worked with, notably, Yalda Osman, Rehmet Hussain, Golnaz Yazdi, Gulalai Habib, Hala Habib, Poran Poregbal, and Froozan Jooya. I benefited from their insights and greatly appreciate their diligence in translating and transcribing the field data. Special thanks to Jennifer Whyte for her assistance with library research; her meticulous attention to references was immensely helpful. Angela Nero's editorial assistance made a difference. I would like to express my gratitude to Roshan Telecommunication and especially to Karim Khoja for his generous hospitality, and to Muhammad Wardeh for his assistance with the dedication. Vincent Carroll graciously took care of my safety and well-being while I was in Kabul. I am indebted to Leila Akhtary, recipient of multiple service awards, for her insights and to Osman Akhtary, a community activist, for his gracious response to all my questions. Thanks to Mohammed Wali and Fatima for their assistance with my research. I acknowledge the generous assistance with references of Moninder Buber, the librarian at Simon Fraser University, and Donald Taylor for his help with copyright issues.

For constructive critique of my work, I owe a debt of thanks to my colleagues and graduate students. I also benefited from the comments received during presentations at national and international conferences and forums. My sincere and deep gratitude to the two anonymous readers at the University of Toronto Press; their valuable critique improved the final product as did the comments from the Review Board Committee. I am grateful to the two journals for graciously accommodating my request to use published articles in this book: *Medical Anthropology: Cross-Cultural Studies in Health and Illness* (Taylor and Frances) and *B.C. Studies: The British Columbian Quarterly* (The University of British Columbia). I owe a debt of gratitude to Douglas Hildebrand from the University of Toronto Press for his encouragement, guidance, and support. It has been a pleasure to work with Lisa Jemison, Stephen Shapiro, and Kate Baltais from the University of Toronto Press: thank you for all your support. This research would not have been possible without the generous funding from the Social Sciences and Humanities Research Council of Canada and Metropolis British Columbia. I acknowledge the assistance of the University Publication Fund, Simon Fraser University.

My deepest gratitude goes to my soulmate and life companion, Aziz. His support, encouragement, and love have been invaluable and boundless. Thanks for your words of inspiration and unwavering faith in my work. I have benefited immensely from my conversations with my daughter Fahreen, an international traveller, who also served in Afghanistan and Pakistan as a physician practising integrated holistic health. My son Zahwil and his family (Monika, Andrew, and Zoe) have been a source of inspiration. Thank you to my sister Yasmin for her moral support. Words of wisdom from my mother have nourished and sustained me spiritually and socially.

In Memoriam

I hereby acknowledge the invaluable work of my Canadian colleagues, **Roshan Thomas** and **Zeenab Kassam**.

Tragically, they were killed by the Taliban insurgents on 21 March 2014, on the special occasion of Navroz (New Year).

This work is also in remembrance of all Afghans and service professionals who lost their lives in the long, drawn-out war in Afghanistan.

May their souls rest in eternal peace.

AFGHANISTAN REMEMBERS

Gendered Narrations of Violence and Culinary Practices

Introduction

For the past two decades, I have been exploring the relationship between violence and social memory and asking what kind of contribution anthropologists can make in this domain. My interest in this subject has personal roots. Along with my family, I was uprooted from my home country of Uganda in 1972. As part of the South Asian exodus, we settled largely in the West: Canada, the United States, and Britain. South Asians were desirable refugees. Having come from a country colonized by Britain (1890–1962), we had been educated under the British system and exposed to a Western way of life. But issues were not as straightforward as they appear on the surface. Our lives were shaped by the colonial policy of social stratification and ethnoracial hierarchies.

Uganda was one of the main destinations for Asians who migrated to East Africa from the subcontinent of India from 1880s onwards. Lured by the prospect of a better life in a new country, the Asians worked hard and gained the reputation of entrepreneurs. At the same time, they were subject to the imperial strategy of racial segregation that "percolated into all aspects of life, beginning with separate toilet facilities for European, Asian and African members of staff in the secretariat, and progressing to residential areas, schools and hospitals, all of which were graded accordingly" (Frenz 2013, 52). Furthermore, the colonial administration confined the Asians (constructed as a homogeneous group) to towns and small trading settlements where they were channelled into trade (Dossa 1994). "Any non-African found living or trading outside a gazette township commits an offence" (Morris 1956, 296; also refer to Adams and Bristow 1978). Being sandwiched between the colonized Africans and the British, the status of the Asians was rendered precarious. Their engagement in trade and commerce was tenuous as they had no political voice. Left to their own resources, each of the Asian communities (Hindus, Muslims, Sikhs, Parsees, and Goans) established its own social infrastructure along with places of worship (Adams and Bristow 1978, 1979; Bhatia 1973; Frenz 2013). When Uganda achieved independence in 1962, close to fifty thousand Asians (2% of the population) had made this country their "home" despite their uncertain legal and social status. Their expulsion from the country by the late President Idi Amin was a result of the anti-Asian sentiment – a colonial legacy inherited by the local African population. Frenz puts it this way: "One could argue that the South Asians became victims of their own success, when colonial legacy and racially grounded nationalism combined to inform political strategies. It was not far from there to the racialist policies introduced by Idi Amin" (55).

Upon migration, South Asian refugees earned the "title" of a model minority: hard working, diligent, and adaptable. Over the years, however, I learned that this dominant narrative was layered. It contained violence in the deeper recesses of life – violence that has yet to be named. My family was split in half. This was not unusual; on the radar screen of the system, we were nothing more than numbers. My sister, my grandparents (who had lived with us for thirty years), and I were separated from my parents and younger brother. We came to Canada while my parents and brother were moved to England to a refugee camp. The separation was painful and difficult, given that the family unit is a source of strength in a foreign environment. Shortly thereafter, my grieving grandmother passed away from shock. Furthermore, my mentally challenged brother (Mohamud) was left behind. There was no room for him in a country such as Britain or Canada, where the refugee/immigration policy is shaped by the needs of the labour market (Li 2003; Razack 1998, 2002). My visit to Denmark in 1973 was revealing. Upon meeting a dozen Ugandan families with disabled children, I inquired as to why they were concentrated in one place. They informed me that Denmark was the only country that accepted children with disabilities. Mohamud died from choking on a banana skin. His life did not matter. My parents were informed of his death through sea mail – three months after the event.

Uprootment and its associated trauma require public acknowledgment on account of the workings of larger forces that affect masses of people. Following Fassin and Rechtman (2009), Das (2003), and Dossa (2004), the term *trauma* used in this book addresses a key question: how is this politically informed experience articulated from the bottom up to effect a structural shift for social justice? Relocating narrations of violence and anchoring them to "juridical-political discourses" is one strategy put forward by Das (393). In their critique of the dominant narrative of Post-Traumatic Stress Disorder (PTSD), Fassin and Rechtman (2) call for an interrogation of the historical and political trajectory so as not to overlook the way in which trauma has been clinically appropriated. In her work on Iranian women in metropolitan Vancouver, Dossa (2004) reveals the subtle ways in which her participants effect a shift away from a clinical to a political and social understanding of this term. While highlighting a bottom-up politicized approach to trauma, I am mindful of the sociopolitical factors that give rise to what has come to be known as *The Empire of Trauma* (the title of Fassin and Rechtman's book).

The Ugandan exodus of fifty thousand South Asians was rooted in the divide-and-rule policy of the British colonial system. Placed in between the Europeans (on the top) and the Africans (at the bottom), the South Asians were rendered vulnerable, as noted above. The receiving colonial countries had some responsibility to set things right. However, this did not happen as their primary interest was to secure labour, including the refugees. A focus on the labouring body compromises one's humanity. Refugees are not considered to be ordinary people; "they are constituted rather as an anomaly requiring specialized correctives and therapeutic interventions" (Malkki 1995, 8).

My experiences of settlement were not smooth as the dominant narrative has it. Four years after coming to Canada, in 1972, I gave birth to twin babies, one of whom died. My physician had not identified that I was carrying twins. Complications arose during the birthing, and one of the babies died. The physician did not show me the baby's face. The body was then used as a test case for research – without parental consent. Not to have an image of a face to *remember* is very painful. I wonder to what extent Malkki's observations are true in my case. This treatment constitutes a form of violence for people who are forcefully displaced.

Ugandan South Asian refugees have their own stories of loss and dispossession among which the intangible issues of identity and cultural heritage loom large. The question is not that of adaptability. Human beings are resilient and can thrive in different environments given the opportunity to develop their full potential. But in our unequal and conflict-ridden world, this is not the case. The logic of race-thinking informs the institutional structures of Canada, a white settler society. Here, people of colour are the Other, a scenario that gives rise to material and epistemic violence. The concerns and aspirations of the people on the social margins, such as the elderly and persons with disabilities, have yet to be addressed in research, in policy, and by the society at large (Dossa 2009; Salari 2002).

War and displacement are phenomena that cause untold harm; the effects are felt poignantly in the inner recesses of life, where they are rendered socially invisible and therefore remain unacknowledged. Insensitivity to suffering and pain in the weave of life results from the distinction we make between lives that are grievable and others that are devalued and ungrievable, to use Butler's observation. To blur this distinction, Butler (2009) calls for recognition of *the precariousness of all lives* (emphasis added). Only then will we realize that "there is no life without the need for shelter and food, no life without dependency on wider networks of sociality and labour, no life that transcends injurability and mortality" (24–5). We would then be more attentive to scenarios such as what it is like for an Afghan woman to sweep the debris from a bomb blast as she goes about her daily chore of sweeping the floor. What is it like for an Afghan woman in Canada to look unsuccessfully and tirelessly for work? And what is it like to feel isolated and socially excluded in a country where one had hoped to build one's future? To make sense of these everyday realities, Butler (2004) suggests that we imagine a world where "violence might be minimized, in which an inevitable interdependency becomes acknowledged as the basis for global political community" (2004, xii–xiii). Precariousness as a shared condition of human life, to use Butler's (2009) phrase, constitutes a starting point for engaged anthropology, where the issue of suffering brought about by social inequality and injustice is paramount. Fassin (2007) puts it this way: "Anthropology is not a matter of art for art's sake, that making things of this world a bit more intelligent, especially when they appear opaque, incomprehensible, and irrational, can make them less unjust, ineluctable, or unacceptable" (22–3).

I define the *inner spaces* as an area where the enduring effects of violence are felt in everyday life but remain hidden on account of the politically constructed situation where some lives are grievable (generally the hegemonic North) and others remain ungrievable (generally the subjugated South). To make this violence knowable, I argue, we need to pay attention to "the voices" of the sufferers'/actors' that include but go beyond language. It is in this context that I focus on social memory, a genre that the women in my study resorted to through narrations of violence and culinary practices.

In today's world, mass displacement of people has become common-place. Three factors may be cited. First, having assumed different forms in time and space, the violence of colonialism (conquer, dehumanize, and rule) is alive and active (Fanon 1963; Thobani 2007). Second, global capitalism has systemically undermined the rights of the marginalized and the racialized Other on a global scale. The US-led post-9/11 "War on Terrorism" is the third factor. As Thobani has expressed it, "The U.S. and its allies launched the War on Terror to reassert their dominance of the Middle East and Central Asia" (2007, 141; 2003). The end result is the suspension of critical engagement where questions on the root causes of social inequalities and justice remain unaddressed. Ginsborg observed (2005, 5):

> The concentric rings of connection, between the material culture of every-day life, larger communities, and the worldwide patterns of consumption and production, have very extended histories. They are the result of long-standing relations between the "North" of the world – its rich and devel-oped regions – and the "South" – its poor and developing areas. The chains of connection that have been drawn across the world fundamentally benefit only one restricted part of it. They do not derive from impulses of equity and solidarity, or from a sense of mutual responsibility. Rather their driv-ing force has been primarily, though not exclusively, economic profit and national power.

Drawing upon data from my ethnographic research in Afghanistan (Kabul, fall of 2008 and fall of 2009) and Canada (Burnaby, BC, 2004–07 and 2009–12), my intent in this book is to make violence in the inner recesses of life knowable through the memory work of women encapsu-lated in the title: *Afghanistan Remembers*. Memory work serves to empha-size two points. First, it is active (hence, the word "work"), and second, it is deployed to politicize the present. In short, memory work is not frozen in time. It generates its own meaning, fostering a dialogical engagement with an audience (reader/listener). It is in this context that individual memories become part of the repertoire of collective memory with its capacity to endure over time. This indeed is part of the struggle to not forget past injustices. I would like to emphasize that women's memory work rarely took place in the context of one-to-one conversation with the anthropologist; it constituted a part of women's everyday lives. For example, the death of a person triggered a conversation that invari-ably included a continuum of the past and the present and at times an unknown future. When Bibi Gul passed away, the women remembered her storytelling skills attracting the attention of the children from the neighbourhood. She had play-acted some of the incidents recalling her family's hiding place in the cellar when the Russians bombed her village. As Farida explained, "It is through her that the children came to know how their lives have changed because of the war (*jang*). Bibi Gul had a swing in the house. It was broken and there was no one to fix it as she lost her husband and her son during the civil war." Her losses made other women recall the violent deaths of their loved ones. Mehrun and Fatima would wash their clothes at the same time. On such occasions, they exchanged stories of hardship and struggles that I was privy to (e.g., the shortage of water and food). They belonged to two ethnic groups: Pashtun and Tajik, respectively. Their acts of remembering created a special bond between them. Leila put it this way: "We share memories of violence and perhaps this is why we get along with all the 'new' people (other ethnic groups) who live in our neighbourhood. We have to work together if we have to build this country." Memory work does not merely evoke the past; it impacts the present.

There were other occasions when memory was invoked collectively. As I walked with the women on their way to visiting kith and kin, they would point to a produce store under construction and relay information on the family that had occupied it in the past. The family had left for Canada. The women then exchanged news on how they were faring and the number of people who had left the country. Many times the walks entailed figuring out who used to live where, their relationships with other families, activities they were engaged in (e.g., work, leadership, and acts of generosity, not excluding conflicts and frictions). Often the conversations revolved around particular places and buildings in terms of what was destroyed during the bomb blasts. A child who had contracted malaria would give rise to a conversation on the potholes – breeding grounds for the mosquitoes. An elderly lady recalled how easy it was to navigate the neighbourhood streets in pre-war times. Now she has a fear of falling; she does not go out very much, stating how this constraint has made her life less joyful. Her comment made other women express concerns about the unrepaired roads, potholes, and rubble – a form of potential mobilization.

Second, survivors of the violence of war recreate normalcy to the extent possible – otherwise I would not have seen women cooking with minimal ingredients, or seeking a cure for a sick family member despite the lack of a support system. As Nafisa put it, "Everybody is poor but we help each other whenever we can." The women sustain their families in the face of great odds in both Afghanistan and Canada. It is through the mundane details of everyday life that the breadth and the depth of harm and suffering caused by violence are revealed. Making it knowable requires an understanding of what Butler (2009) calls "precarious lives," fundamentally a shared condition of human life. The issue, then, is differential distribution of "precariousness," whereby ungrievable lives "are made to bear the burden of starvation, underemployment, legal disenfranchisement, and differential exposure to violence and death" (25).

It is not my intention to homogenize the life situations of the participants of this study. I have taken the women's narratives and formed a tapestry that maintains singular colours and textures leading to the formation of a whole, but the tapestry is not complete. It continues to be woven as Afghans remember how wars have changed their lives. Afghanistan is militarily occupied. The US/NATO plan to withdraw the troops by the end of 2014 does not mean that peace will prevail. There is no talk of peace – rather, the foreign troops are training an Afghan military force. Does not militarization give rise to more violence that, invariably, makes its way into everyday life? The question that needs to be asked is: What impact will indigenous militarization have on the lived realities of Afghans? Will their children go to school? Will they have shelter over their heads? Will they have enough food to feed their families? Will they be in a position to celebrate religious occasions? Will it be safe for them to go out? Will they be able to socialize with kith and kin? Will they have access to health facilities? Will they be able to nurture spiritual and moral lives? These questions are at the core of what makes us human and how we can live meaningfully, as opposed to mere survival from one day to the next.

Through the memory work of women, I seek to bring to light the not-quite-articulated knowledge that exists within in-between spaces (here and there, the local and the global, the individual and the collective). Ong (1995) observes that anthropology needs to reflect on the postcolonial situation whereby we increasingly live inside, outside, and through the East-West divisions (368). The voices of ordinary women engaged in memory work across borders (homeland to diaspora) could help to establish epistemological and methodological points of intervention into the literature on the violence of war. As Scheper-Hughes and Bourgois (2004) have argued in the anthology *Violence in War and Peace*, it is through the study of violence at its broadest level (sociopolitical and intimate) as well as within the depths of human life that we can begin to address the crisis facing humanity in today's world. On another front, Das (2007) calls upon readers to witness violence rather than merely observe it. This can be accomplished through the deployment of alternative methodologies, one of which is the language of everyday life.

My own voice is not absent in this work. I have presented my interpretation of the data, while leaving room for other perspectives. My voice of advocacy and research accountability is also emphasized. I consider this stance to be important in a world where the violence of war is endemic. It is in this context that I have attempted to make a case for the potential of memory work to effect a paradigm shift – a shift that would lead to acknowledging rather than "forgetting" the immense suffering inflicted by the violence of war. _Forgetting_ here refers to an intentional act of not remembering for political reasons.

harm and suffering inflicted by the vio-
Meintjes et al. 2001). Exemplifying the
ng their worlds in the midst of devasta-
eir status in times of social disruption is
nbraces care work and nurturing within
diate families. The women in my study,
ved in fostering kith and kin ties rup-
ng task as women's lives and bodies are
litical agendas. As Abu-Lughod has ex-
stcolonial world, women have become
visions of society and the nation" (also
; Azarbaijani-Moghaddam 2004). These
symbols and visions are also at work on the bodies of refugee women, as de Alwis has observed: "The refugee woman is 'frequently produced as a cipher for all that was (temporarily) lost as well as what must be preserved for the future; the purity of displacement [is] imbricated in her moral purity'" (in Giles et al. 2003, 3). Commenting on the situation of Afghan women, Hunt notes (2002, 119):

> Not speaking out against the representations of Afghan women as passive and oppressed serves to legitimize war and divide women across cultures. As Zillah Eisenstein states "western feminism is used by the global telecommunications networks – TV, e-mail, CNN news – as well as the film industry to define a colonialist/imperialist narrative that reconfigures barriers between women across the globe" (1996, 141). The depiction of American women as free and liberated compared to depictions of Afghan women as restricted and oppressed serves to divide women and limit the possibility

of uncovering the ways in which women in both countries are silenced and objectified in definitions of this conflict.

Malathi de Alwis (2004) reinforces the above points, noting how women reclaim their sense of identity through "multiply layered constructions of 'home'" by invoking sites over which they have control: the kitchen and the sleeping quarters. Identifying the significance of domestic utensils, de Alwis notes how these "invoke a particular space within the 'home' – the kitchen which thus gets produced, in this context, as the ultimate core of the 'home'" (226). Women's desire "to recreate a semblance of a familiar domestic world" is tied to the reconfiguring their homeland (226). Within this larger expanse, I argue, women attempt to recreate their identity of motherhood. This observation is reiterated by Ross (2001) and Todeschini (2001). In their respective works on the South African Truth and Reconciliation Commission, and the atom bombs dropped in Hiroshima and Nagasaki (1945), both authors note how women's self-definition of motherhood is politicized to reveal the effects of violence and injury on humanity. In the same vein, de Alwis (2001) makes a case for the power of tears ("the language of organs"). As a tangible signifier of suffering and grief, she argues, tears legitimized the protests of the mothers against state brutality: "The production of tears is such a complex and concatenated bodily fluid, as an essence of 'motherhood,' proved to be one of the most powerful forms of 'body speech' that was mobilized in the public(ized) practices of the Mothers' Front [Sri Lanka] and the discourses they engendered" (198–9; also see Barlow 2004). Anchored in the socially valorized status of motherhood, Afghan women reveal the complex ways in which they combine housework and wage work. As Farida explained, "We have to cook, look after our children and do all the housework; at same time, we have to earn money to feed our families." The women in my study expressed the view summarized as "if we stay home, we can perform multiple tasks," including social engagement with kith and kin. Their desire not to split their work into two realms – domestic and public – suggests an alternative way of "being mothers." For a cross-cultural ethnography, refer to *An Anthropology of Mothering* (Walks and McPherson 2011).

In this book, I identify the social location of Afghan women – a location that is both national (Afghanistan) and diasporic (Canada). Afghan women remember, not unlike those others who have experienced the violence of war and displacement (e.g., Hesford and Kozol 2001; Giles et al. 2003; Giles and Hyndman 2004), what the world has forgotten, namely, that the violence and social disorder in their country cannot be exclusively attributed to the internal dynamics of power. The superpowers, as I show below, are implicated throughout the course of the country's recent history. Through women's memory work, Afghanistan remembers (*Afghanistan hemesha ba yadi medashta bashd*).

Recent History of Afghanistan: A Summary

As a buffer state, Afghanistan has always attracted the attention of outside powers. Its strategic location as a landlocked country has made it into a gateway for the Middle East, and South and Central Asia. At issue is the play of geopolitical factors prompting contending powers to invade and occupy the country, especially when regional politics – as opposed to a strong centralized state – has been the order of the day. When the Soviet Union invaded Afghanistan in 1979, at the height of the Cold War, the United States stepped in and fought a proxy war by funding and arming the mujahideen (resistance fighters). Their original goal:

> was not so much to oust the Soviet forces as to make them pay a heavy price for the invasion. "The maximum achievement would be to make the cost of the Soviet presence extremely high so that they would learn a lesson and be discouraged from trying in other more important places ... Furthermore, as early as 1982, the CIA and the State Department knew that the bulk of their assistance was going to Islamic fundamentalist groups of the Mujahideen that were anti-American or had ties to anti-American groups in Iran." (Khan 2001, 9; cf. *Globe and Mail* 1993; also see Jiwani 2006; Stockton 2004)

Massoud, the leader of a mujahideen faction, had this to say: "As always, it is the question of money. Western companies are interested in the resource-rich territories of northern Afghanistan. They also want to penetrate the adjacent countries of Central Asia: Tajikistan, Turkmenistan, and Uzbekistan" (Saikal 2006, 222). The question that was not asked is: How will the civilians fare in the superpower rivalry unfolding on the soil of one of the poorest countries in the world? According to the GDP 2011 criteria of the United Nations, Afghanistan ranks 106 out of 194 countries.

With the departure of the Soviet Union in 1989, Afghanistan was abandoned, but not without being turned into an armed camp. The bulk of the military support was given to the hard-line factions who fought for power: "Kabul now became the scene for a power struggle between four main armed groups, Dostum's Junbish-e-Milli militia, Rabbani and Massoud's Jamiat-I Islami, Hekmatyar's Hizbe Islami, and the largely Shi'a Hizbe Wahdat" (Johnson and Leslie 2004, 23; Shahrani 2002). It was at this time that seventy-five per cent of Kabul lay in ruins, and "tens of thousands of civilians fled their homes" (Johnson and Leslie 2004, 23). The Taliban from the south of Afghanistan (Kandahar), many of whom were trained in religious madrasa in Pakistan, moved into the capital. At first, they promised to bring in law and order, but they changed course the moment they made more territorial gains by 1995. While they imposed brutal medieval rule in the name of Islam, suppressing the rights of women to a level that can be described as extreme, the world looked the other way. In fact, the United States, in alliance with the regional powers (Pakistan, Saudi Arabia, and the United Arab Emirates), supported the Taliban, thus ensuring its expansion and grip on power. The United States and its allies shared a common ground: "to contain the Islamic Republic of Iran and prevent it from gaining influence in Afghanistan and in the newly emerged mineral and market-rich region of Central Asia" (Saikal 2006, 223). Washington maintained silence over the Taliban's violation of the rights of women and the minorities (especially the Shi'as), and over the large number of non-Afghans who joined the ranks of the Taliban. Among such persons was the Saudi millionaire by the name of Osama bin Laden who set up the network of al-Qaeda. A reciprocal relationship was established between bin Laden and the Taliban: he provided monetary support and brought in jihadis (fighters), while the Taliban gave him sanctuary and the support he needed to set up terrorist camps from which he launched the 9/11 attack on US soil.

This incident led to the 2001 US-led military invasion and occupation of Afghanistan. Forming an alliance with NATO, the United States launched an international War on Terrorism. The rationale for this war is based on the long-standing representation of the West as a beacon of democracy and freedom in the world (Jiwani 2006; Thobani 2003, 2007). Its gendered script is couched in terms of women's oppression by their culture and religion, epitomized by the burqa. While ignoring, or minimizing, "the existence of the various forms of patriarchal practices and misogynist violence prevalent within the modern societies of the west" (Thobani 2007, 228), the latter has presented itself as the liberator of non-Western women. The image of the oppressed Afghan woman is entrenched in the Western psyche; her "oppression" is attributed to Afghan culture, tribal tradition, and religion by the global stakeholders (Ayotte and Husain 2005; Khan 2008). The issue is that "they [the non-Afghans] will not accept responsibility for how they are implicated in the plight of Afghanistan and the conditions of Afghan women" (Adeena Nazi, president of the Afghan Women's Association, personal communication, Toronto, Aug. 1997, quoted in Khan 2001, 7).

The above discussion reveals the erasure of the recent history of Afghanistan, muting the role of the United States and its allies in bringing about the social malaise in the country. More importantly, the concern is non-recognition of the precariousness of life, here (the West) and there (the East), muting the question: "What politically can be made of grief besides a cry for war?" (Butler 2004, xii). My intent in this book is to show that in the wake of this historical and political amnesia, *Afghanistan Remembers*. And this act of remembrance captures violence in the inner recesses of life. Unnoticed and rendered invisible, this form of violence reveals the depth of injury and suffering inflicted by war. For anthropologists, this understanding is linked to the commitment to engaged work directed towards social justice and creating space for conversation across socially constructed boundaries. In exemplifying the family, the community, and the nation, women play a key role in remembering from a site that forms the core of social life – the hearth – along with the narratives that it evokes. For Afghan women, the hearth represents the life-giving substance of food as well as a means through which they remember "the family dinner table," in the words of one woman. Another woman put it this way: "If we do not have a hearth/fire we cannot cook. If we do not cook, we cannot eat. If we do not have food, there cannot be a family." The hearth reminded the women of their strength and resourcefulness as homemakers and mothers. Extending this meaning to fostering social relationships, Rehmet, a participant in this study, stated, "Even if we do not have anything, if the fire is burning we can at least boil the water and serve tea to visitors." The above observations reveal women's anchorage in the space of the home – a space that has been disrupted by the violence of war. Many of my study participants had a tiny space for cooking as opposed to a full kitchen as they had in pre-war times. It is through the hearth that they reclaimed a sense of home – a site of stability despite its feminization. De Alwis (2004) cautions us that during times of disruption, we need to keep in mind various articulations of home so that we can problematize this unit. In this vein, a reclaimed home with hearth as its centre evokes nostalgic memories in the form of "absent belongings, mourned relationships and quotidian trauma" (227). It is in this context that I discuss the political and social value of memory (remembering) poignantly expressed through two means: narratives and food within the space of *there* (Afghanistan) and *here* (Canada).

Anthropology of Social Memory (*Khatera*)

Anthropologists have added their voices to the burgeoning literature on social memory. By way of a contribution, they have delineated the close, bottom-up connections between memory, violence, and social suffering. This focus reveals the workings of violence at a level not captured by official remembering. It falls "within the ambit of what Richard Werbner describes as 'rights of recountability' – 'the right, especially in the face of state violence and oppression, to make a citizen's memory known and acknowledged in the public sphere'" (1998, 1, in Ross 2003, 27). Rather than a mere recollection of past events, memory work holds the promise of creating new subjectivities within the spaces of devastation where it is revealed more acutely. For example, in her work on the Partition of India, Das (2003) shows how the memory of violence can exist in the form of poisonous knowledge in everyday discourse. We may note that suffering cannot be exclusively recalled in language. Writing about the horrifying effects of the structural violence of AIDS in South Africa, Fassin (2007) argues that memory is embodied. It exists as history in the flesh. Noting how bodies remember, he observes, "What they reveal more profoundly are traces of an everlasting past" (xvi).

Memories of violence are not isolated or singular. They are told over a period of time to particular audiences. Such was the case with the women subjected to the nuclear bombings in Hiroshima and Nagasaki. Silenced by the official discourses that sanitized and medicalized their bodies, the women chose to bide their time until they achieved the socially valorized status of motherhood. Through the act of remembering, they gave a human face to their suffering. They conceived of the bomb as embodied in their wombs to give the message that atomic suffering is a threat to the human race. Their memories of suffering reflected "bonds of love, friendship, and solidarity that bind families and communities together" (Todeschini 2001, 148). It is in these communities of affect that harm can be acknowledged as Ross (2003) has argued with reference to her work, *Bearing Witness: Women and the Truth and Reconciliation Commission in South Africa.* She underscores "the presence of an empathetic listener on the grounds that the narrator-witness pleads for attention even when the story carries no hope, only the recognition of damage and the limitations of effort to heal" (5).

Ultimately, memory work contributes to shifts in our interpretation of history: "As they [recollection of events] are launched into the flow of collective memory they have a chance to endure over time, multiplying available perspectives on the past" (Waterson 2007, 66; also see Antz and Lambek 1996; Bourguignon 2005; Daniel 1996; Das 2007; Johnson and Leslie 2002). Waterson goes on to state, "The drive not to allow the forgetting of traumatic events or past injustices is a moral drive" (2007, 66).

Two themes are highlighted in this discussion: (1) memories reveal the workings of violence that otherwise remain unknown, and (2) there is a need for research accountability in an interconnected and unequal world. My ethnographic research with Afghan women has revealed the importance of these orientations showing that memories do not always function in isolation. They achieve depth and poignancy through such means as narratives (*qesa haa*) and food (*ghezaa*).

Narratives (Qesa Haa)

Narratives/narrations (active process) complement memory work at two levels. First, they infuse life into the work of memory. As a human activity existing within a web of relationships, narratives provide flesh and bones to the acts of memorialization. The imperative to tell stories is greater in times of social malaise and disorder. Narratives then enhance the process through which we come to know how the social disorder (structural violence) becomes entrenched in the inner recesses of life. Second, narrators assume the presence of a listening audience to whom they make a claim to acknowledge and validate their memorialized experiences in the cause of justice (Fassin 2007; Ross 2003). I wish to emphasize women's use of the testimonial mode, an act of self-witnessing capturing the lived realities of a cohort with similar experiences.

Memorialized narrations can then lead to a reflexive listening and reading of the resultant texts that Dorothy Smith (1999) refers to as "active." Texts are like "speakers in a conversation; that is, though deprived of the possibility of hearing and responding to us, as nonetheless present and active in 'speaking' to us as our reading activates them. Our reading operates the text; in our reading it becomes active" (135). The challenge is to listen to the narratives (texts) in a manner that brings to life the memories of suffering along with the reconstitution of lives. My analysis of the memorialized narrations of violence has been guided by their potential for engaged anthropology. Focus on the latter prompts us to remember with our participants and not for them, while not overlooking the workings of power that cause undue suffering.

Food (Ghezaa)

Food is more than nutrition, and more than a substance that satisfies hunger. It encompasses realms that are social, political, cultural, and spiritual. As an everyday activity, culinary practice has meaning for us; it lends itself to creativity and imagination. The provision, preparation, and consumption of food constitute part of our way of life, defining who we are as culture-bearing beings. However, in the contemporary world of global capitalism, our lives are subject to commodification understood as a process of co-optation "to the power of neoliberal managers and market-centered governance into ever greater spatial, social and political arenas" (Lind and Barham 2004, 48).

Another school of thought highlights gaps in the market-centred system that people at the local level respond to through acts of resistance. With varying emphasis, both approaches consider food to be an important arena for capturing larger developments. This is because food is a tangible way to explore "wider social cleavages, and political and cultural change" (Smith and Jehlicka 2007, 397). Second, food takes us into the lane of history where we can explore continuities, change, and ruptures, a prime example of which comes from Lind and Barham (2004). In their work on "The Social Life of the Tortilla," these authors chart the transformation of the tortilla from a staple food of the Mayan and Aztec people to a fast food of the Americans. Rather than adopting a linear narrative of co-optation of food by "the increasingly powerful criteria of the market metaphor" (58), they illustrate the symbolic power of food. Third, food has social lives. Before it appears on the shelves of the supermarket or in the carts of vendors, food passes through places, changes hands, and is subject to cultural, symbolic, and institutional norms.

Observing that greater attention is given to the political economy of food (Lind and Barham 2004), scholars have turned their attention to the politics of resistance to highlight an integrated framework where the material, social, symbolic, and cultural dimensions coexist. Writing on post-Soviet Uzbekistan, Rosenberger (2007) shows how the Uzbeks unsettle the state project of nation building through bodily awareness of "gnawing hungers." As eating is an everyday activity, food "remains within people's control to bestow meaning on it, even though it is highly constrained by the political and economic forces of the nation"

(341). Following a similar line of thought, Smith and Jehlicka (2007) question the linear narrative of global capitalism assumed to have taken root in Poland and the Czech Republic in the post-Soviet era. Using the metaphor "biographies of food" to emphasize liveliness, the authors reveal alternative ways in which food is produced and consumed. They note that we must take into account what food tells us about the larger world, namely, "that our futures are not fixed by the seemingly pervasive and insistent characterizations of development as contained, controlled and predestined by a narrow and frequently destructive version of how economy and society might function" (408).

The above examples show that we first need to question an exclusive focus on food as a material item for satisfying hunger and providing nutrition. Thinking of food as simply being distributed to the disenfranchised population worldwide does not acknowledge its symbolic and cultural value. Second, the commodification of food with the sole focus on profit-making rarely takes into account a situation of food deprivation, the brunt of which is borne by people in the global South. The anthropologist Paul Farmer (2003) has called for health to be included as part of human rights. Should not food be placed under the same category, provided we recognize its cultural and symbolic value within particular milieus? In short, should we not exercise caution so as not to reduce chronic scarcity to mere satiation of hunger as this stance compromises our humanity? There have been some developments at this end. Under the banner of food insecurity, Chilton and Rose (2009) call for a right-to-food approach based on two components: "social and economic environments that foster human development, and to provide food to people in an emergency or in circumstances when self-provision is beyond their control" (1204; see also Kent 2005, 2010, 2011). While this strategy forms part of the UN Declaration of Human Rights (1948), with its emphasis on the right to adequate food and a decent standard of living, it falls short at multiple levels. Marchione and Messer (2010) identify three issues. First, the right to food cannot be isolated from other rights such as the right to livelihood, health, social services, and land, along with the right to participate in political decision making. Second, in the case of chronic hunger, food should be made available to countries, groups, or individuals in a culturally respectful manner. Third, observing that food is distributed unfairly and in a manner that is ineffective, the authors call for the establishment of a self-reliant food system on a global scale.

An anthropological perspective directs us to explore these aspects from the bottom up in relation to the lived realities of people. In the case of protracted violence, as is the situation with the female Afghan subjects of this study, the multifaceted nature of food is brought into sharper focus in the light of the everyday struggles for survival. And this focus is tied to memory work of critical importance, as it is through the active interface of food and memory work, I argue, that the disruptions of everyday life can become knowable. This understanding makes it possible for us to identify the political economy of violence as defined by the research subjects, not excluding the process of recovery. As the women struggle to procure food for their families, they remember at the same time. And their acts of remembrance enhance the sociocultural dimensions of food.

My approach to the subject matter of food is not in the tenor of perpetuating the association between cooking and gendered subordination. Drawing upon the works of Duruz (2005) and Gvion (2006), I show that, during times of crisis, women are in the forefront of change. And this change is effected through food. In an illustrative case study of two women's "culinary journeys" in the multicultural settings of England and Australia, respectively, Duruz shows how women through an "economy of exchange (a complex one of food, ideas, experiences, knowledge, caring) foster intercultural interactions" (2005, 66). On a different front, Gvion illustrates the ways in which Palestinian women in Israel combat poverty and resist oppression by drawing upon "gender-based stocks of knowledge" (2006, 299). It is in this vein that I advance the argument that the culinary knowledge and practices of Afghan women form part of memory work subverting the official discourse of the "inner chaos" in Afghanistan.

Memory, like food, is a social phenomenon, and remembering the past as present brings into sharper focus social injustices. The question that arises for consideration, then, is what do we do once we understand the inscription of violence in the inner recesses of life – inner because it is not noticeable? As an anthropologist, I suggest an engagement with the recent disciplinary trend towards accountability in research. Accountability amounts to recognizing, for example, that disenfranchised persons have social and cultural lives that go beyond the satiation of hunger.

Food as an everyday act of performance and memory as a means of making the past present are each powerful tools in their own right. The act of performance/practice highlights enactments of violence as well as attempts at recovery. It draws our attention to "the liveliness" of food – how it is procured, prepared, and consumed in everyday life. Performing and remembering bring into sharper focus the occurrence of everyday violence. This is because both acts are embedded in the quotidian worlds where they are reactivated and reconfigured in relation to specific situations. It is through the social consumption of food, not the mere act of eating, that we affirm our identities as culture-bearing beings. Like narratives, food reveals the multiple ways in which people rebuild their lives within spaces of devastation.

Signature of War: Spaces of Devastation

Districts in Kabul contain well-built renovated homes standing alongside battered ones. Both types bear the signature of war. Built by middle-income families (including the returnees from Western countries), the renovated homes are either rented to *angrez* (foreigners) at $2,000 to $3,000 per month, or subdivided into one or two bedrooms and rented to local Afghans for Afs1,000/$20 to Afs2,500/$50 per month. Owners of battered homes do not have the financial capacity for renovation. As such, they continue to live in what were once five-bedroom homes, now reduced to one or two bedrooms with or without a kitchen. Physical spaces of devastation are noticeable everywhere. Holes in the walls of the courtyards, torn trees, rubble, charred buildings, landmines, and the general upkeep of the homes speak to, in the words of one woman, "violence that you have not been subjected to." Potholes and gutters reflect unrealized reconstruction. Rather than allowing them to become static in the form of taken-for-granted reality, the women keep alive the lived memories of these spaces of devastation. The holes in the buildings along with the scars (visible and invisible) on the bodies of people tell the story of violence and injustice. The women who speak through the pages of this book collectively convey the message: "We must not forget the destruction of our country and of our lives. The world must understand the long-lasting and therefore deeper impact of violence."

Central Questions

Research in a war-ravaged country evokes key questions: How does violence translate into the everyday lives of people? What does it mean to lose one's world? How do people reoccupy spaces of devastation? What role can anthropologists play in uncovering everyday violence (*khushunate rozmarah*) that otherwise remain unknown and, therefore, unacknowledged? These questions are interrelated. Once the violence of war is unleashed, it "attaches itself with its tentacles into everyday life

and folds itself into the recesses of the ordinary" (Das 2007, 1). I argue
that memory work – an active and fluid process – as a construct can address these questions not in the form of definitive answers, but more in
the way of initiating a conversation between research participants and
the stakeholders, and among the stakeholders, transnationally. I show
in this book that knowledge of the past, and the process of recounting
it, are connected in space and time through such means as narratives
and food. Anthropologists, with their penchant for documenting thick
description, can become part of this flow of remembrance; anthropologists can bring to light memories that otherwise remain buried. Through
their work – engaged or critical – anthropologists can evoke the presence of a listening audience. Ross (2003) puts it this way: "The absence
of an empathetic listener, or more radically, the absence of an *addressable
other*, another who can hear the anguish of one's memories and thus
affirm and recognize their realness, annihilates the story" (3, original
emphasis; cf. Felman and Laub 1992; also see Feldman 1991).

In sum, this book attempts to show the potential of memory work to
make knowable violence in the deeper recesses of life. At the centre of
my study are ordinary women whose acts of remembrance are barely
known to the outside world. They remember what the world has forgotten, namely, that violence has a long history embedded in external forces
not of their making. In the case of Afghanistan, the complicity of Russia,
the United States, and its allies must be brought to light if we are to write
a different kind of history – one where issues of social justice and human
dignity are given central space.

Organization of the Text

In chapter 1, I provide a mapping of ethnographic research in relation
to two main sites: Afghanistan (*there*) and Canada (*here*). Adopting the
premise that methodology and epistemology are interconnected, I present field notes and stories/vignettes, respectively, to show how I engaged
with bottom-up memory work revealing violence in the inner recesses
of life, not excluding attempts at recovery. I map my research trajectory:
in Afghanistan, it meant doing research in a battered city; in Canada,
it meant recognizing a second moment of violence, namely, retraumatization in the country of settlement. I make a case for the potential of
memory work in evoking the attention of a listening audience, a stance
grounded in engaged anthropology. I discuss my entry into the field informed by two factors: (1) my identity as a South Asian Muslim refugee

from Uganda, and (2) my research in a war-torn Muslim majority country. I note that both aspects require negotiation.

Chapters 2 and 3 contain testimonial narratives of Afghan women in their homeland (*there*: Afghanistan) and in the country of settlement (*here*: Canada). Through the memory work of women, I engage in a reading of the text in terms of what is said and what remains unsaid. I argue that it is within the space of the unsaid that we can begin to interrogate the unequal relationships of power between the global North and global South. I conclude with some observations on the potential of the intertwined relationship between memory work and narratives to reveal the impact of violence in the inner recesses of life. What does it mean to undertake the task of preparing everyday meals with minimal ingredients in the homeland? What does it mean to experience ruptured food biographies in Canada? These questions form the subject matter of chapters 4 and 5. I show how the everyday activity of the provision and consumption of food captures the processes of loss and recovery. In the concluding chapter, I revisit the themes of the book and discuss their implications for an engaged ethnography.

In this book, I have paid close attention to gendered memory work with the conviction that this construct allows us to understand the effects of violence in the deeper recesses of life. Once we realize the impact of embedded violence generationally, we may be motivated to work towards mitigating it through discipline-based accountability.

Accountable and engaged anthropology is increasingly given a central place in works that deal with issues of violence, social suffering, and injury and harm (see Low 2011). The theoretical challenge is to address the local realities and see how they interface with global capitalism, the order of the day. Underpinning the latter is the neoliberal ideology with its emphasis on austerity budget cuts that has left a large number of people globally without the basic necessities of life, including self-dignity and human rights. It is to highlight this larger narrative that I have resorted to memory work. The act of remembering allows us to travel in space and time and establish linkages with the worlds that are otherwise considered disparate (*here* and *there*). This point requires emphasis as the global media and the stakeholders attribute the disorder in Afghanistan exclusively to internal forces encapsulated in the image of "the Taliban." Representing Western hegemony, the United States, as well as Canada, has not acknowledged its complicity in destroying the infrastructure of Afghanistan and wounding its people. As discussed above, the United States and its allies fought a proxy war with the Russians and then abandoned Afghanistan after having turned it into an armed camp. Following the tragic incidents of 9/11, the United States invaded Afghanistan on the pretext of introducing democracy and liberating the women from a supposedly oppressive culture and religion. Currently, the United States/NATO is in the process of withdrawing its troops – a process accompanied by the creation of an Afghan military force. Does this not constitute further militarization of the country that is bound to lead to more violence and more suffering? The trajectory of events needs to be remembered as it has contributed to causing undue harm and injury to the civilians within spaces that are barely noticed: the inner recesses of life.

It is through memory work that the women evoke the attention of a listening audience. Researcher, readers, and advocates can become part of this audience. Through the bottom-up memory work of women, rendering the past into the present, we come to understand how violence weaves itself into everyday life. We may then be motivated to work towards creating a more peaceful and just world – a project that forms the core of engaged anthropology. Hopefully this project will also help us to see that the socially constructed boundaries (epistemological, territorial, and cultural) between Afghanistan and Canada are blurred – global recognition of which can lead to a paradigm shift towards a more equitable distribution of resources that can come about through "forging links among those who refuse to participate in the either/or projects of 'us' and 'them'" (Giles and Hyndman 2004, 314).

1
Epistemology and Methodology

Since 2006, I have conducted field research among Afghan refugees in Burnaby, Canada, and also briefly in Quetta (August to September 2007), the largest city and the capital of the province of Baluchistan, Pakistan. Focusing on gendered experiences of displacement and resettlement, I explored the effects of a double moment: trauma/social suffering in the home country and retraumatization in the diaspora accompanied by efforts towards recovery. It was at this juncture that I recognized the importance of memory work, as the women I conversed with not only recalled past events but reconfigured them in the present to make sense of their suffering. I then asked them, "What was the originary moment of violence?" They answered, "Go to our country (*mamlakat*) and see for yourself." Prompted by the women, I made two trips to Afghanistan, in the fall of 2008 and the fall of 2009, respectively. By way of a beginning, I lay out the context of my research: homeland (Afghanistan/*there*) and diaspora (Canada/*here*). My goal is to engage in reflexive methodology that invariably includes questions on epistemology, namely: How do we witness acts of violence? Going beyond mere observation, witnessing is a palpable activity that entails seeing, hearing, and feeling the impact of violence contextually; it evokes the question of what do we do once we have a politicized understanding of this violence? The first step is to understand how the violence of war is woven into everyday life, where it is normalized and remains hidden.

"The World Must Not Be Allowed to Forget"

It was on the fine day of 28 August 2008 when my plane descended into Kabul. As we reached the ground, the majestic mountains gave way to the sight of myriad military helicopters stationed at the airport. There were two main kinds: US/NATO choppers equipped with the latest technology and the older, battle-worn remnants from the time of the Soviet occupation (1979–89). The helicopters served as a tangible reminder of the long-term and continuing violence that has plagued the people of Afghanistan. As I drove along city streets accompanied by an armed guard, I observed military convoys speeding by while the rest of the traffic came to a halt. They, the foreign troops, had the right of way, as I found was the case with many things in the country. I wrote in my diary: "This country is at war but with whom?" Surely over one hundred thousand US/NATO troops, would not have been deployed to fight the Taliban/insurgents? Saikal's observations came to mind: "The attractiveness of Afghanistan for foreign powers has been variously attributed to its rich mineral resources, its infrastructure development potential and its ability to house military bases"; equally important is "the country's pivotal location in the heart of Central Asia" (2006, 6). This script remains unarticulated and is barely acknowledged in the global circuits of power (see Ayotte and Husain 2005; Daulatzai 2006, 2008; Donini et al. 2004; Johnson and Leslie 2004; Khan 2008).

The helicopters that I saw at the airport did not recede into the background. Not a day went by when I did not hear the loud sounds of the choppers on their way to military bases in other parts of the country. Rather than being mere objects doing their work, the helicopters capture the politics of *khatira*: who remembers, and what modes are employed to capture the politics of remembering and forgetting. Since 2001, Afghanistan has been in the news, globally. The reference point is the brutality of the Taliban – the regime that was toppled by the United States and its allies on the pretext of liberating the women and introducing democracy to a "backward" country. This saviour script is deployed to advance the vested interests of the West noted earlier. The fact that the troubles in Afghanistan began with the Soviet invasion in 1979 with the United States close at its heels is rarely mentioned in the global media and remains buried for the world as a whole. But the people subject to everyday violence and suffering remember – and along with them, Afghanistan remembers through the scars on the body politic. The message conveyed is to this effect: "the world must not be allowed to forget." In their role of exemplifying the family unit, women (*zanaan*) bear the brunt of violence, and as such they engage in active memory work through such means as testimonial narratives and culinary performance. Their memory work speaks to the experiences of their cohort, their families, reconstituted communities, and increasingly, to their country (*mamlakat*). "We hope that our children will work for the country's good" was a recurring theme in their accounts.

Militarized Peacekeepers

Walk down the streets of Kabul on a given morning and you will see young and older men going to work. On foot, on bicycles, and in motor vehicles, these are the people who are rebuilding Afghanistan in small ways following over three decades of war and conflict. The women work alongside men; whether at home or in offices, they, too, are engaged participants. However, the everyday struggles of ordinary Afghans are barely noticed as their work does not lead to either the accumulation of capital or production on a scale that matters in a global capitalistic system. Yet, it is these people who have nurtured and sustained their families in trying circumstances, not knowing when they may be the targets of bomb or rocket attacks, let alone other forms of violence that are barely acknowledged. Looking even more closely, you will notice the anomalous situation of children (*atfal*) working on the streets. These children encapsulate the scars of war on their bodies and also symbolically on that of the sociopolitical body. You will also see girls and boys going to school. They embody the future (*ayenda*).

Seventy-five per cent of Kabul was destroyed during the "civil war" from 1992 to 1996. You will notice SUVs, mini-vans, and military tanks choking the streets, thereby making it difficult for the local people to use the space that is rightfully theirs. The commuters are the expatriates (private entrepreneurs, staff of the international aid community, and the military). Employed by foreign corporations, agencies, or governments, they, too, are going to work. The expatriates have come to believe that they are rebuilding a devastated country and are "helping" the people of Afghanistan to reconstruct their lives. Their work is facilitated by the UN Bonn Agreement of December 2001. Set up to establish an interim government and an infrastructure, the agreement contains a fundamental contradiction shortchanging the people of Afghanistan: it promised to restore peace in the midst of waging the War on Terrorism: "It [the Bonn Agreement] certainly represented a new era of international engagement in Afghanistan, but it was an engagement that took place in the shadow of a massive military campaign in retaliation for the events of September 11, 2001" (Johnson and Leslie 2004, 157).

The above constitute notes from my field diary. They bring into relief a major issue of concern to the anthropology of violence, namely, social insensitivity compounding the originary experiences of violence.[1] Yet, as Das (2007), Dossa (2009), and Ross (2003) have noted, people subject to suffering deploy alternative means to give voice to their experiences through such means as storytelling (Dossa 2004, 2009; Todeschini 2001), the language of silence (Ross 2003), the language of the body (Fassin 2007), the language of everyday life (Das 2007), and social memory (Degnen 2005; Antz and Lambek 1996). In doing so, the sufferers evoke the attention of a listening audience in their search for social justice (Das 2007; Fassin 2007; Low 2011).[2] I would like to consider pertinent questions that ethnographers would be inclined to ask: How do we acquire a palpable understanding of the impact of war on families, kinship networks, and communities? How do we address the paradox of the perpetuation of affliction by institutions set up to do relief work in the first place? How do we speak with and not for our research participants to validate their context-specific experiences? What is the relationship between memory work and social justice? How do we bear witness to violence as opposed to being mere observers? These questions formed the baseline of my methodology, linked to epistemology with its premise of the social construction of knowledge. The collection of data is not a neutral activity; it is embedded in the dynamics of power that need to be worked through and negotiated.[3] In short, my research was not unproblematic. When I visited the homes of the women, there were times when my participants would ask me to come back as their daughter or son was not around. In the words of one woman, "We want them to know our stories. Otherwise how will they know what we have gone through?" The opposite scenario also prevailed. There were times when the women did not share their stories with me because their son or their daughter was present. In this case, they wanted to spare their children the pain and suffering they had experienced. At times, I waited for close to an hour for a neighbour to join us. These occurrences cannot be dismissed as insignificant as my participants decided who would witness their stories, at what point in time, and in what context. Research can be a form of witness whereby we can acknowledge not only the violence of war but also how participants position themselves so that their stories/life experiences are remembered not by one person but by an audience.

Crossing Boundaries in a Divided City

From the early stages of my research in Afghanistan, I realized that my work would take place in a divided city. And, certainly, I was caught in a maze crossing borders back and forth. I stayed in the compound of an

international aid agency for security reasons, but my daily travels took
me to the homes of the women. As I talked to the women and observed
their everyday lives, I realized how little they were understood by the
service organizations claiming to do grassroots–level work (Moyo 2009).
Allow me to present an example to illustrate this insensitivity – the politics of recognition. During a health session on malaria, the women were
advised to get mosquito nets to protect their families. In response to
one woman's observation that the cost would be an issue, the health
instructor suggested that she shop around for an inexpensive one; a
second woman expressed concern about the cost of transport, while a
third woman noted that her busy schedule (housework and home-based
wage work) would make it difficult for her to shop. The Afghan instructor clearly understood these issues, but did not have the leeway to assist
the women. Having been trained by an international (German) donor
agency, she was expected to follow foreign guidelines.[4] Daulatzai, an Afghan anthropologist, takes issue with how little the lives of Afghans are
understood by aid workers and institutions poised to assist them. She
further notes how a limited set of analytical concepts such as gender,
patriarchy, and a particular rendition of Islam fail to explain "how gender has been inflicted by violence, war and occupation and subsequently
what work war and its forces have performed on social institutions, family structures and individual subjectivities in Afghanistan" (2006, 306).

These concerns evoke two interrelated questions: How can we make
the experience of violence knowable? And, "How does the availability
of a genre mold the articulation of suffering – assign a subject position
as the place from which suffering may be voiced?" (Das and Kleinman
2001, 5). These questions informed my research at four primary districts
in Kabul: Shar-e-Naw, Shash Darak, Khair Khana, and Kota Shangi. Research was also carried out in Taimani and Kate Parwan. My research at
these sites was facilitated by an international aid agency called Baraka
that operated or had contacts in these districts. The study participants
saw my research as an opportunity to share their stories and life experiences with kith and kin – one opportune moment among others when
they could engage into memory work in their words: "what life was like
and what it had become." While I was concerned that my presence with
a driver/bodyguard (*negahban*) could potentially endanger their lives,
this was not the case. My participants assured me that their own homes
were safe both for them and for me, too. They explained that the insurgents had no reason to target women's homes surrounded by the rubble of war. As one woman expressed it, "Our homes have already been

destroyed and many lives have been lost by the wars in Afghanistan. They [the Taliban/insurgents] do not have anything to gain by coming here." It was only because of the insistence of my research assistant (Yalda) that I took a guard – many times a driver. She, too, was not concerned about endangering the lives of the research participants. Her fear was that we might become the unfortunate target of a bomb blast on our way to the women's homes as we had to travel on the main roads to get to our field sites – roads frequented by the military convoys.

I sought to understand the impact of the violence of war on the everyday lives of people. Knowing full well that this form of violence is not easily knowable, as Das (2007) and Ross (2003) have noted, among others, my goal was to see how women remembered and lived with violence – a project that calls for ethnographic research. People on the ground resume their everyday lives despite issues of insecurity. Afghanistan is not a war zone in the literal sense of the term. As noted earlier, my research participants were keen to share their stories with me. I did not assume that my research would necessarily have a negative psychological effect on my participants, including the research assistants. Such an assumption undermines the resilience of the survivors. I soon learned that the everyday lives of women embedded in memory work (not severing the present from the past) was one means through which they sustained their families' well-being despite constraints and losses resulting from protracted conflict. The women in my study echoed Kadar's observation: "her story needs to be told so that it will not be forgotten" (2005, 88).

Conducting sustained research in a city subject to frequent bomb blasts proved to be challenging (Nordstrom and Robben 1995). Oftentimes, I had to turn back from my destination of the day because of warnings of violence and unrest. At other times, potential participants cancelled their appointments at short notice also for security reasons. I did not consider these interviews to be unrealized. The cancelled interviews speak to the crises that Afghan women and men experience daily.

As a Muslim ethnographer and a South Asian refugee from Uganda with a functional knowledge of Hindi and Gujarati (my mother tongue), I had prepared myself for the problematic duality of being an insider/outsider. I had hoped that my insider status would work to my advantage in terms of my receptivity. This was not the case. Despite my understanding of Muslim etiquette and practices (greetings, gift giving, rituals, and dress code), I had to establish my credibility through Baraka. Only then did the women feel safe in inviting me into their homes. As they came to know me as "a privileged sister from Canada," they introduced me to their neighbours and peers. One introduction led to another, and during the course of my research, I met women from several different walks of life: mothers, donor agency staff, female ministers, and professional women. Yalda, my research assistant whom I met through an aid agency, worked closely with me. She continued to conduct research interviews for four additional months after I returned to Canada. The data we collected together and the data set that she collected on her own have been integrated into the body of this book. I also worked with Rehmet, a social worker from Baraka.

While I had thought that my Canadian background would hinder my entry into the homes of the women, this was not the case. Despite the presence of ten thousand Canadian troops, they were not visible; they were shadowed under NATO which my participants equated with "the Americans." In fact, they made frequent references to the Americans, disappointed that they have not done much for the people of Afghanistan. The international image of Canada as a peaceful country has credibility in Afghanistan.

The open-ended interviews encouraged women to tell their own stories. Guided topics included life before the Soviet invasion, the impact of the wars on their lives, community support, internal and external displacements, everyday lives, observance of festivals, health and crisis situations, the preparation and consumption of food, the status of women, home-based waged work, and aspirations for the future. Fifteen service providers (Afghans and non-Afghans) from different agencies participated in the study. I engaged in participant observations at the homes and neighbourhoods of the women, agency-based programs, and the streets of Kabul. The observations of the latter were made from the comfort of the van as it was not safe to walk for long. Depending on the choice of the participants, the data were collected in Dari or Pashtun and transcribed into English by the research assistants. In this study, I have attempted to capture the words and the worlds of the women/the narrators.[5] This undertaking is critical in a situation of remembering the violence of war. Citing Felman (1992, 69), Kadar (2005) observes, "The effect of trauma [not in the medical sense] can only be undone by constructing a narrative, reconstructing history, and essentially 're-externalizing the event.' The short version of the effect is: This re-externalization of the event can occur ... only when one can articulate and transmit the story – literally transfer it to another outside oneself and then take it back again inside" (86). It is in this vein that the women in my study shared their narratives with the researcher along with their kin and kith. As in my earlier work

(Dossa 2004), my voice as an ethnographer is not absent. I have built on the contexts provided by the women so as to provide geographical breadth and historical depth, to use Paul Farmer's words (2003), to the extent possible.

Ethnographic research is challenging as it requires us to work through time-consuming logistics, exercise sensitivity, be cognizant of social and cultural milieus, document the nuances and complexities of human life, engage in participant observations, work through dilemmas and contradictions, and write up our data ethically. In a country where violence is a daily occurrence, these components did not fall into place easily. There were many times when interviews did not take place owing to bomb blasts or security alerts at my end, too. There were other occasions when I could not conduct scheduled interviews owing to crisis situations such as a sick child or a panic attack by a mother whose son had not returned from school. For my research participants, the possibility of a child being kidnapped or hurt in a car accident or a bomb blast was very real, as these are common occurrences. However, these were not unrealized interviews, but speak loudly to the crises that the women experience in their everyday lives; these are the spaces of devastation. Ironically, these spaces are not noticed by the outside world, and the political messages that they convey remain buried.

In a war-ravaged country, it is difficult to undertake long-term research. My short stay meant that it was impractical for me to "pitch my tent" in a local area. I stayed in the compound of an international aid agency. My living quarters rendered me an *angrez* (foreigner) implicated in creating a divisive social life. The *angrez* and the local Afghans live in two different worlds. The former (comprising the military, the entrepreneurs, and the aid agency staff) are well protected by armed guards in their SUVs, and they enjoy amenities that many feel are earned as a result of them risking their lives in a war-torn country. Quite the opposite, the Afghans (with the exception of the upper class) struggle on a day-to-day basis. They receive no protection from the bomb blasts, and they survive on a bare minimum. Afghan men who earn their living as guards risk their lives daily to protect the *angrez*. Each day, as I crossed the border from my life of comfort (with air conditioning, hot water, and abundant food) within the walls of the expatriate compound to the local areas, I felt both uncomfortable and helpless for those around me who did not share these luxuries. At the same time, I was also aware that I was putting my own life at risk, as I could have been hit by the frequent bomb blasts that occurred during my everyday travels within the city.

Doing Research in the Diaspora (Canada)

Diaspora scholars have highlighted the multiple meanings this term has assumed since its original conceptualization as forced displacement from a homeland (see Agnew 2005; Castillo 2012; Hua 2005; Lopez 2012; Mountz and Wright 1996; Pasura 2013; Ray 2004). In this age of global migration, the term *diaspora* evokes transborder identities (Joseph 2013), reconfiguration of gender and kinship (Lopez 2012), the reconstruction of home and intimate relations (Boehm 2012), the formation of hybrid identities (Duruz 2005), and the politics of food (Mankekar 2002): "Understanding diasporic formations can help us comprehend the relocation and community-making of those people who were previously oppressed and colonized, as well as those who are forced to – or choose to – stay put back home" (Hua 2005, 191). Despite its potential to enrich lives through the acquisition of what I call border knowledge from two or more countries, diasporas capture a paradox as they "exist in tension with the norms of nation states and with nativist identify formations" (192). Joseph (2013) puts it this way: "Knowledge, skills and cultural resources of migrants that are underutilized in the receiving nations have detrimental social and economic effects on migrants' communities and the nation-state" (35). Faced with prejudice and hostility from the host society, diasporic subjects/migrants reconfigure their lives under constraints and structural limitations (Pasura 2013; Soto 2012). Drawing upon the case study of transnational Mexicans in the United States, Boehm (2012), for example, illustrates the extent to which the arm of the state reaches what are otherwise intimate relations of kinship and gender. Defined as "illegal," the migrants are not able to cross the border "freely" to visit their relatives in rural Mexico. Their social exclusion makes Boehm raise the question of who would protect the rights of families located "here" and "there," a point of view highlighted by Castillo (2012).

The literature on diaspora reveals two interconnected themes: (1) the lives of diasporic subjects are embedded in contradictions and tensions arising from their social, economic, cultural, and religious exclusion from the host society – an exclusion characterized as racism; (2) diasporic subjects actively negotiate the realities of their lives despite structural constraints. These observations are highlighted in the following examples. Citing the case study of Mexican immigrant girls in California, Soto (2012) illustrates the ways in which they reconstruct a strong sense of being Mexican in the United States; the irony is that they are considered as less Mexican in their homeland. Being marginalized and racialized, their identity is born of pain and a sense of loss. Writing on the care work of Japanese-Filipino women, Lopez (2012) makes two points. First, care work gives these women a higher status compared with their previous work in the entertainment industry. Second, this new status is informed by the Japanese government's need for care of its aging population. The paradox is not lost to the reader: the feminized work of Japanese-Filipino women continues to be part of "the global care chain" (264). In the case of the Malaysian migrant women in Australia, Joseph (2013) illustrates her research participants' use of "their multiple educational and cultural resources in the (re)making of their global and work identities" (34). Informed by the discourse of whiteness and economic liberalization, these women are compelled to lead compartmentalized lives. While they adopt the mainstream market norms of self-management and individualism, they mask their cultural and religious practices: "These identity strategies were not valued within their workplace and so they silenced these markers" (35). In his work on transborder identities of Zimbabwean migrants to Britain, Pasura (2013) argues that the hostile reception from the state reinforced the migrants' transnational religious ties to their homeland, serving a political purpose. It is within this religious-oriented transnational space that the Zimbabweans critique the values and the norms of the British society: "Diasporic configurations [then] can be seen as an alternative space of belonging and reference point for establishing collective identities in a society that constructs them as the Other" (38).

My research on Afghan women in Canada does not differ substantially from the thrust of the argument presented in the above works, namely, migrants experience tensions and contradictions arising from socioeconomic exclusion in their host country notwithstanding a less than amicable environment in their homelands. The latter may be a function of economic displacement, political situation, religious persecution, or war and violence. Second, drawing upon cultural and social resources from transnational/borderland spaces, migrants actively engage in remaking their worlds with women playing a special role in their status as bearers of culture and tradition, construed dynamically and contextually. As de Alwis (2004) has observed, "Women transform threatening spaces into familiar places or territories through material and representative practices that endow them with value and belonging" (215).

In short, diasporic theorizing provides an alternative perspective to the traditional concepts of bounded cultures and tightly structured nation states. Furthermore, "It can help one to understand the social world resulting from displacement, flight, exile, and forced migration" (Hua 2005, 196). As I show below, the Afghan women in Canada in my study used the medium of memory work to capture the above themes.

As I began to explore this double moment of violence (trauma in the home country and retraumatization in the country of settlement), not excluding the bottom-up gendered recovery work, I was faced with the challenge of identifying participants who would allow me to conduct ethnographic research (participant observations, conversations, story-telling, and semistructured interviews). My concentration at one field site in Canada provided me with the opportunity to get to know people in the area over a period of time, a method identified by Malinowski (1922).[6] As I came to know the women on such occasions as shopping on the main street of Valley View, volunteering at a community school, and attending programs (especially ESL classes), they invited me into their homes with my research assistant. Service providers as well as my research assistants were also instrumental in establishing contacts.

In the early stages of my research, the women informed me that there was not a single family (*famil*) that was spared the trauma of war in Afghanistan. In other words, everyone had memories of war that they narrated: loss of lives, erosion of livelihood, and tortuous stories of escape. Moreover, none of the participating women came directly to Canada; their escape route included one or more countries. Two popular neighbouring countries of migration were Pakistan and Iran. From there, some of the refugees went to India or Russia depending on their kin-based connections. Others moved back and forth between their country of migration and Afghanistan, hoping that things would improve in their homeland. None of the families had envisioned permanent exile. Their arrival in Canada was an act of providence as per the explanation provided by a participant: "Imagine a lot of fish in the river. There is a bridge that they are all trying to cross. Only some can make it. It depends on luck. Others keep on swimming, hoping that they will find a place that they can call home."

Mapping Ethnographic Research

I identified two criteria for participation: motherhood (a valorized self-defined status discussed above) and residence in Canada for between four and fourteen years.[7] The first criterion matched that of the women in Afghanistan. The majority of the women I met considered their primary status to be that of mothers, despite having careers and professional designations. My second criterion was based on the need to collect data on Afghan women's lives in Canada, for which a minimal period of four years gives one the opportunity to comment on issues such as social services, housing and employment, educational opportunities, the politics of identity, social relationships, and the practice of Islam. The criterion of four years was also meant to engage Afghan Canadians on topical issues pertaining to Canada and the world at large – one way to recognize their sense of belonging. The semistructured questions, life stories, and conversations focused on life in Afghanistan, experiences of migration, the process of settlement in a new country, everyday life, training programs, waged work and work in the house, food preparation, intergenerational relationships, health, the practice of Islam, and any other current topics that the women identified as important. I have stayed with the stories, choosing to cover depth rather than breadth. As is the case with the data gathered in Afghanistan, I have fictionalized all names.

I trained and worked with four student research assistants in keeping with the criteria of my grant. The first two assistants, Poran and Golnaz, were Iranian Canadians. I later met and hired two Afghan student assistants, Froozan and Hala. I benefited from insights provided by Gulalai, an Afghan service provider. As was the case with my research participants in Afghanistan, my participants came from different ethnic backgrounds: Pashtun, Tajik, Hazaras, and Baluch. The women in my study suggested that I de-emphasize their ethnicity and focus on presenting them as Afghans because "the wars (*jang*) in our country (*mamlakat*) have changed everything" (Rehmet). When I asked them if they had preferences for particular names to maintain anonymity, they suggested that I could include other Muslim names. They felt that this would avoid repetition of common names. Importantly, "we are part of the Muslim *Umma* (community). Our struggles require that we work together as a global community" (Farida, an Afghani service provider).[8]

I had the opportunity to interview twenty providers who serviced settlement and community-based programs as professionals and volunteers. My contact with service organizations also led me to the homes of women who live in low-income housing in Valley View (fictional name) in Burnaby. In this study, I have endeavoured to give central space to the memory work of women expressed through the mediums of narratives and food. Given this focus, my first task was to connect with the participants at a level where their memory work is validated. This means recognizing participants as producers of context-specific knowledge, a topic that has received attention in critical and feminist anthropology. Henrietta Moore (1996) raises the question: "What is social knowledge for?" She suggests that this question does not require a response but a series of interrogations "along the lines of what sort of knowledge is produced, for whom and for what reason" (2). Armbruster, an advocate of ethical and accountable research, also notes: "The imperative to study people in ethically guided, that is, empathetic and respectful, ways is a form of valuing and validating how someone is to be known and what types of knowledge should merit the label 'anthropological'" (2008, 3).

Identifying our position as researchers is crucial. Who we are, and what motivates us to undertake research at particular sites are issues that require some thought so as "to locate the agency of the others, and thus to develop new forms of social engagement that ensure a radical departure from the earlier situations of anthropologists speaking for the others" (Moore 2000, 15). My own story of the political economy of displacement has been a catalyst for this study. I cannot forget that our lives, built over three generations in Uganda, came to an end within a span of ninety days – the time period given to the South Asians to leave the country. Gradually over time, I began to understand the political economy of displacement rupturing the fabric of social life. This point needs emphasis, as economics is used as a yardstick with which to measure the success of immigrants/refugees. Colonization, imperialism, and the military complex underpinning global capitalism have been identified as the primary forces that lead to the disruption of lives globally (Thobani 2007).

Storytelling/vignettes were the medium through which I was initiated into my field site at Valley View, where I have been doing research among Afghan refugee women since 2006. The first story connecting *here* and *there* comes from an Afghan service provider, Sadaf, who assisted me in establishing contacts with the women. Intertwining her narrative with those of other refugees that she works with, Sadaf talked about the struggles of everyday life: looking for work, settling children into school, learning about social services, experiences of racism, maintaining health and well-being, and securing housing. She also brought to light issues of identity, belonging, self-dignity, and being a Muslim in a Western country. As she highlighted issues in each of these sectors, she depicted life in Afghanistan by dividing it into two parts: what it was like in the pre-war period, and how it has changed through wars. For example, she referred to women as being secure and protected by their families and respective communities. However, she stated:

> This is before the war (*jang*). Whether they were working on the farm, in the house, or in an office, they were part of a large family with extended kinship ties. But during the war, things changed. Women's lives were at risk as the protective shelter was no longer available. Our lives were destroyed (*kharab*) by various wars.

Sadaf then related how wars brought about a situation that "affected women badly. They were married off as fathers were scared that their daughters would be kidnapped or that they could not feed them as families became *poor (gharib) and poorer*" (original emphasis).

Sadaf's comment echoes Kandiyoti's critique of the hegemonic and static narrative of Afghan women as being oppressed by their culture and religion. She notes, "The dynamics of gendered disadvantage, the erosion of local livelihoods, the criminalization of economy and insecurity in the hands of armed groups and factions are analytically distinct phenomena, yet their effects combine seamlessly to produce extreme forms of female vulnerability" (2005, 13).[9]

Sadaf went on to say that "Afghan refugee women have a very difficult time in Canada. They are not able to move forward as they face numerous barriers." With this observation, Sadaf gave her own example of how her credentials from the University of Kabul were not recognized despite the fact that she is fluent in English. "I ended up working with the refugees as if I cannot do any 'Canadian work,'" she noted. Sadaf's story, both personal and testimonial, reveals two related themes: the double moment of violence, and along with it the connection between *here* (Canada) and *there* (Afghanistan) – a connection that we need to recognize if we are to present a more complete picture of the recent history of Afghanistan. This is the reason why Afghanistan remembers – it seeks to correct the distorted history where the Taliban is the reference point for the political erasure of the post-1979 memories of violence.

The Saviour Script

My second initiation came through the story (profile) presented by a Caucasian service provider, Mona. Mona is an energetic and dedicated worker. She talked about how much she wanted to help "the refugees as I had a difficult time growing up. Since I was young, I decided to go into service work. The job has its challenges but it is very satisfying for me. We have programs that benefit women, men, and children." She then provided a list of services such as counselling, English as a second language (ESL), and health and nutrition. She observed:

> When refugees (*mahjerin*) come to Canada, they have a lot of trauma from their home countries. They come to a new country and they do not know how things work here. We help them to get acclimatized and to learn what it means to live in such a wonderful country as Canada. We are all immigrants here. We need to learn to live together. Canada is a safe place – a heaven for refugees. There is no violence here. This is the country where they can build their lives and make progress.

In the above vignette, *here* (*inja*) and *there* (*anja*) are imagined as two different spheres. *There* is the place of trauma caused by war and violence. *Here* is the place where this trauma is addressed through the trope of a better life in a country envisaged as "heaven." The assumption that there is no connection between the two countries needs to be addressed.[10] In fact, violence over there is attributed to the workings of power and politics over here (Khan 2001). Likewise, Giles and Hyndman have noted, "Nationality, gender, religion, caste, and cultural context situate people unevenly within a web of relationships that transcend political borders" (2004, 6). In other words, the script of the political economy of violence and displacement is not remembered over here/transnationally. Equally important is the usage of the term *refugees*, a term that my research participants did not use except for legal purposes. In the context of service provision, the Otherness of the refugees is reworked to make them like "us" – acclimatized to the Canadian way of life to summarize Mona's not atypical views. However, even if the newcomers desire to become like Canadians/mainstreamed, their Otherness is not erased due to systemic racism and Islamophobia. Commenting on this point, Razack et al. (2010) note, "Critical race scholars across North America have linked imperial and colonial racism to the conceits of modern liberal states, which purport to be race neutral, colour-blind, and even postracial, while masking, reproducing, and even reinforcing historical inequalities" (xvii).

It is equally important to problematize the social category of "refugees." Generically, refugees are persons who seek asylum in another country owing to their persecution and displacement in their countries of origin. Malkki (1996) informs us that the category "refugees" needs to be interrogated in the wake of humanitarian interventions arising from the mass displacement of people globally. These interventions are carried out in a manner that is dehumanizing and dehistoricizing, creating "a context in which it is difficult for people in the refugee category to be approached as historical actors rather than simply mute victims. It can strip from them the authority to give credible narrative evidence or testimony about their own condition in politically and institutionally consequential forums" (378). Here, then, we have a situation of not remembering the circumstances and the conditions that displace people in the first place. This critical omission is not without consequence as it creates refugees as persons without history and agency – a situation that absolves global stakeholders from responsibility for wars and violence that take place elsewhere.

Like their counterparts in Afghanistan, the Afghan women in Canada remember, and their memory work is politicized. This places the onus on us, the anthropologists, to engage into more complicated understandings of local realities. Towards this end, I present the third story (two vignettes) to introduce the themes explored in this book: memory work and its value in bringing to light violence in the inner recesses of life along with the interconnectedness between *here* and *there*. In feminist praxis it comprises, "political action which conceives of differences as linked, if unequal, and which upsets commonplace markers of social, cultural and political identity" (Giles et al. 2003, 6).

VIGNETTE ONE

When we first came to Canada, my husband, Esmail, was depressed. He was imprisoned and tortured in Afghanistan. They would not let him sleep and they beat him up for the two months that he was in a cell. They let him go once they came to know that they had the wrong man. When he came home, we left our house that night. We did not want to risk them coming back and taking him again, or even taking one of my sons. You can never tell. You see the mujahideen bombed Kabul and used rockets. They did not come to our homes. With the Taliban, it was different. They came and took family members and our goods. When we left Afghanistan and went to Pakistan, we thought we would return. We had hardly taken anything with us. But we could not go back as the situation in Afghanistan got worse. We came to Canada. We wanted to work hard and start all over again. My husband [Esmail] began to have nightmares. We took him to the

doctor. He gave him pills. But Esmail did not get better. He started throwing things in the house. I called the hospital and told them that it was an
emergency. They ignored us. Somebody told me to create an emergency
situation. I called the hospital after a few days and told them, "Esmail has a
knife (*kaard*)." They came right away. He got the treatment he should have
had months ago. (Maryam)

VIGNETTE TWO

Housing is a real problem. They do not understand that we have large families. My neighbour has four children. There are two girls and two boys. They
put them all in a one-bedroom apartment: a mother and her children. The
father was martyred in Afghanistan. They have been telling their worker
that they need a bigger place. Who listens to them? Their sixteen-year old
girl, Farah, cut her wrists. Only then they were moved to another place with
a two-bedroom apartment. (Adila)

Both vignettes reveal violence in the weave of everyday life where it remains unacknowledged until it surfaces at critical junctures (a husband
"having a knife" and a girl cutting her wrists). Esmail and Farah embody
memories of the violence of war. Rather than healing in a new place,
they encounter the second moment of violence: retraumatization. It is
this double moment of traumatization that connects the two countries:
Afghanistan and Canada. A caveat is in order. Trauma in the homeland
and retraumatization in the country of settlement does not exclude the
process of the rebuilding of lives. The women in this study showed resourcefulness in sustaining their families under difficult circumstances;
they also displayed keen political awareness. For example, following an
introduction to the multiple recreational programs offered at the community centre, Rehana noted, "We first have to think of where our rent
will come from and what we will eat. We cannot 'eat' these programs."
Further conversation revealed the issue of structural barriers that she
encountered in looking for work or career opportunities. Note the reference to "we" that other women used as well, showing that they speak in
a politicized voice. Likewise, taking a similar stance, women in Afghanistan observed that "liberation" does not mean getting rid of their burqas
capitalized upon by the United States and its allies prior to the invasion
of Afghanistan. The women I spoke to in Valley View desired education
and jobs, not available on a large scale to socially excluded groups such
as immigrant women (Agnew 1996; Dossa 2004).

   In this book, I argue that the violence of war becomes entrenched in
the inner recesses of life. In order to make it knowable, we need to pay

attention to how it is "voiced" by the narrators. Early on in my research in Afghanistan and Canada, I observed that the women (my research participants) resorted to memory work to make sense of the present and to reconstitute their lives. Having endured prolonged war, they recalled the originary moments using testimonial narratives, where one person speaks for her cohort.

The women did not exclusively verbalize the multiple ways in which violence had become part of their everyday lives. They remembered through culinary performance, as well, a subject that requires close attention. As an integral part of our lives, food reveals the workings of violence more poignantly. Memory work, and the mediums through which it is expressed (narratives and food), has epistemological significance as it highlights lived realities (the enactment of everyday violence) that otherwise remain socially invisible. It is within the space of these realities that we come to know of the harm and injury caused by the violence of war along with the attempts at recovery within spaces of devastation.

Memory work (*khatera*), narratives (*qesa haa*) and food (*ghezaa*) are social phenomena that can direct us to ask the question long posed by anthropologists: What makes us human? Alternatively, we may ask: What are the forces that compromise our humanity? These questions remain unanswered in the light of the glaring inequalities and the injustices that have become part of the global social order. In sum, through memory work from both *here* and *there*, I have endeavoured to reveal its potential to bring into relief a deeper understanding of the workings of violence in the weave of life where it is normalized. Making this form of violence knowable can be one small step towards creating a just world. It is this knowledge that makes us realize the precariousness of our lives at a fundamental level.

In Afghanistan, the complicity of the superpowers in bringing about violence (not absolving internal and regional dynamics of power) is forgotten and replaced with the narrative of the internal disorder attributed to the "uncivilized Other." As an ally of the United States, Canada's complicity in prolonging violence in Afghanistan is likewise not remembered in the global corridors of power. The hegemonic narrative in circulation among the global stakeholders is framed to depict Canada as the saviour of the people from the global South, perceived as a chaotic place of violence. *Afghanistan Remembers* (*Afghanistan hemesha ba yadi medashta bashd*) may then be considered as a point of intervention into this hegemonic narrative. Encapsulating family, the women are at the forefront of memory work (an active process), imagining a world free of social injustice and violence. Diasporic remembrance, as Agnew (2005) has argued, enhances memory work. As one remembers, one takes into account two sites: homeland and diaspora.[11] Living in the latter is challenging not because of the inadaptability of human beings to adjust to a different environment, but because of the insensitivity within the political systems, telling us that "Others" are not like "us" (Quesada et al. 2011). Bottom-up memory work, in the homeland and in the diaspora, brings into relief the suffering that war and conflict engender within the core of our existence: everyday life with the hearth as its centre.

By highlighting the memory work of women in the inner recesses of life, I have endeavoured to create some space for reflexive remembering along with attentive listening. It is through these avenues that memories can become active. Dorothy Smith's comment on "active" texts applies to memory work. She notes: "I mean to see them as being like speakers in a conversation; that is, though deprived of the possibility of hearing and responding to us, as nonetheless present and active in 'speaking' to us as our reading activates them. Our reading operates the text; in our reading it becomes active" (1999, 135). Smith observes that active texts are enabling as they lift the words and the scenes from the text and give them life. Memory work performs a similar task. It creates a position of remembering *with* the participants (conversational mode) and not *for* them (appropriation mode).

I hope that by the time readers have finished this work, they will have a clearer understanding of the existence of violence in the inner recesses of life where it is barely visible; they will be able to place women's memory work within political and historical contexts; and further, they will be able to engage in reflexive moments, situating themselves in the discussion on violence, memory work, and social suffering. Towards this end, I have adopted the premise that methodology (as opposed to mere methods) and epistemology are interrelated. This premise takes us into the heart of the question: How do we blur the socially constructed boundaries between us and them? Forming the core of engaged anthropology, this question has informed my methodology and analysis of data.[12]

2

Testimonial Narratives

Remembering in the Homeland

For people who are subjected to prolonged violence, as is the case with those in Afghanistan, there is a collective narrative that Beverley (1992) refers to as "testimonio." Testimonio is characterized by an urgency to communicate an issue and a need to articulate "a problematic collective social situation in which the narrator lives. The situation of the narrator in testimonio is one that must be representative of a social class or group" (95; cf. Dossa 2004, 13–14). Testimonio is integral to active remembering where the past and the present are fused: "We do not eat fruit because our garden was burned." "I got married early to the wrong person because my father was killed by the Taliban." "My children do not have shoes and warm clothes for winter as we lost everything during the [civil] war." "We only have naan [bread] and tea for breakfast. We used to have cream, cheese, cookies, and fruit." Testifying reveals how violence can become normalized because of societal misrecognition.[1]

Memory work evokes the originary moments of violence. *How did I find myself in a situation unimaginable prior to war?* This is the question that underlines women's everyday struggles, such as providing food for their families and ensuring that their children can attend school. Memory is recovered rather than frozen in time. And individual accounts of violence (which do not exclude recovery) are underpinned by testimonial narratives of: *What happened to our country and our people, and how are we reconstituting our world?* Testimonial memory work acquires poignancy and meaning through the means of telling and retelling, remembering, and recalling. This act, I argue, takes place on the plane of structural vulnerability as a result of prolonged violence (see, e.g., Quesada et al. 2011).

It is on this plane that a deeper level of connection takes place between individual recall and a collective recall.

Keeping in mind that testimonial narratives recall the life situation of a single author that, in the final analysis, represents a collective situation, I begin with the narratives of two women, Amina and Hamida.[2] These women represent two different scenarios that contain themes high-lighted by other narrators in this study. Amina encapsulates a middle-class family's descent into barely visible poverty; Hamida encapsulates a poor family's descent into ultra-poverty. Both women engage in memory work to reveal the depth of their losses and attempts at recovery. Their accounts are based on originary moments of violence: How did we arrive at this situation where our lives are shattered in ways that the outside world does not recognize? This critical question leads to a need to tell the story of how violence in war is enacted in everyday life. Below, I also present individual experiences of other women on the plane of struc-tural vulnerability to show how they contribute to the telling of a collec-tive narrative, not excluding retrieval of voice.

The above account simultaneously informs the framing of the next chapter where I discuss how memory work in the inner recesses of life takes place within the space of the diaspora. While the focus of the pres-ent chapter is to establish a connection between the individual and the collective, the next chapter will build on this theme and include an ad-ditional dimension: interrogating the socially constructed entities of *here* and *there* to show that they are, indeed, connected. The implications of testimonial narratives in the light of this interconnectedness will also be discussed.

Meet Amina and Hamida. They live in Khair Khana, a well-known district housing various renovated residences many of which are occu-pied by the *angrez* (foreigners). Living in battered homes of one or two bedrooms, the Afghans receive no protection. The marked contrast is a reminder of the life that Afghans once enjoyed, recalled by the women in terms of before the war and the aftermath. The "before" was not be-reft of struggles.[3] But it did not cause the pain and suffering that have become part of their everyday lives. Encapsulated by the phrase social suffering, the "after" may be read at three levels. The first level comprises the originary moments of violence that, in the words of one woman, "split my life into two." Harm and injury should evoke compassion and remedial measures. But this does not happen. Instead, this second level consists of societal indifference (Fassin 2007). Third, people subjected to violence do not merely survive. They reconstitute their lives even within spaces of devastation. These intertwined levels lead to the telling of testimonial narratives. Here, singular memory work maintains its distinctiveness within a larger tapestry. I have focused on depth rather than breadth in the interest of staying with the narratives to the extent possible as opposed to moving on.

Originary Moments of Violence

We have lost everything (ma huma chezi khod ra az dast dadem).

– Amina

Amina lives in a home battered by bomb blasts and gunshots by the Taliban. It was once intact, and reveals the life that she enjoyed with her husband, their three children, and her mother-in-law. Currently, it has two rooms. The other four are unlivable. My visits to her home for interviews/conversations or for salaam (greetings) took place in the mornings before she left for work. Invariably, she would be seated on a mat with her three children (aged thirteen to sixteen) with books spread out: "I want my children to get a good education. I teach them reading and writing. They are good children. I worry that they do not get enough nutrition." Her limited budget does not allow her to purchase meat and fruit: "I am the only person earning [money]. My husband died during the time of the Taliban."

Her everyday struggles to provide for her children make her remember the past (*gozashta*). She worries that her children do not get enough food. She worries that she does not have savings for medical treatment in case they fall sick. She worries that she does not have enough money to buy them shoes and uniforms for school. She worries that her children have to walk to school in the dust in the summer and in the cold weather in the winter. Kabul is infamous for its dust that has to be reckoned with:

> I was so happy (*khoshi*) in my life and I was passing it in a good way. We were living in Khair Khana in a house we shared with my father-in-law's family. My husband was an employee of a government agency and was getting a good enough salary which was enough for our daily expenses. At that time, I was also teaching in one of the state schools close to our house. So the income we were getting was good enough for our children's school supplies, uniforms, and their other expenses. We had our own house. We had six rooms, two kitchens, and two toilets, a garden, and almost ten chickens.

War had a bad effect. I had a complete life with everything. The wars had so many negative effects on our life. During the Taliban regime, we lost everything such as our house, and garden, and chickens, so many, like a chicken farm. They burned our garden, destroyed our house, and were very bad with our men. Like they were saying to the men, "Let me measure your beard with a lamp glass and if it is less than the size of the lamp glass then you will be punished very hard; if not, then we will release you and nothing will happen to you." These are also the bad effects of the Taliban. My children were deprived of school as they [the Taliban] were really against education and school. As I mentioned, my husband had a good job and was earning enough income; but he lost his job as the Taliban even closed most of departments, agencies, and offices, and after a while he died due to a Taliban bomb in our area.

[After his death (*marg*)] my mother-in law was so aggressive to me. She was fighting with me and saying very bad words to me without any reason. Anyway, she died, and God bless her. The Taliban had brought a very strict and bad regime to the Afghan people, and so most of the people died due to these situations. I stopped teaching because women were not allowed to work outside of home. Now we are living in the same house, which was destroyed during the Taliban regime, and it now only has two rooms, a kitchen, and a toilet. But the rest of the rooms and everything else has been burned and destroyed by the Taliban. I am teaching at the state school that I used to teach at before and get about Afs4,000 per month. You know, such an amount is not really enough for us because the cost of living in Afghanistan gets higher and higher, as well as my children go to school, so they need school supplies, uniforms, and some good foods and fruits to get energy and be able to continue learning. Because if you don't have good energy or good meals then you will lose energy and there won't be a way anymore to survive and continue living. The worst effect I got from the wars is my mental problem (*jigarkhoni*), which I have received from so many wars in Afghanistan. Like, I am most of the time nervous, shouting at my children, thinking a lot, worrying, and being concerned and other things. So these were the bad and negative effects of the wars in Afghanistan.

Amina recounted this part of the story in one breath, highlighting discontinuities. Her battered home is an everyday reminder of the tragedy of violence. Recall her words: "Now we are living in the same house, which was destroyed [by] the Taliban." She describes her "before life" as a happy one. They had a home and their children were getting a good education. The "after life" is beset with losses, dispossession, and erosion of their livelihood. She is concerned about her children's education as she is not earning enough to provide for them. She feels that they are undernourished and that this will impact their learning abilities. Her remembrance of war and violence is embodied in the form of trauma ("my mental problem").

During my subsequent meetings, including participant observations, I asked her more questions about her everyday life in an attempt to grasp what it is like to reoccupy a place that has been devastated. She recounted her struggles of living as a widow with young children. She feels that she is carrying a heavy burden, doing all the house chores and earning a livelihood. She has gone back to her teaching job except that the salary she earns is small (Afs4,000/$80 a month).[4] She worries a lot about her financial situation.[5] I understood Amina's concern about feeding her children well. On three occasions, she packed the following for their lunches: naan and cheese, naan and beans, naan and eggs (*tukhm*). She wished she could include meat and fruits – part of the staple diet in pre-war times.

Her concern about nutritious food is also linked to a past experience. When her husband died, there was not enough food (*ghezaa*) for her children. The memory is scripted into her everyday life. She referred to this experience as part of "the negative and bad effects of the wars in Afghanistan":

> The wars were a very bad shock to every Afghan person. Everyone around the world knows that the most risky and unsafe country is Afghanistan. So I was really shocked during the wars, especially when my husband was killed under the Taliban's bombing. It was really a bad shock to me that I became a widow and had three children left to me. I didn't know how to feed them. I mean, I was not working and we had already finished the food we had at home. So I was worrying about where to find food from and how to nourish my children as they were small and saying, "give us food, Mom, give us food (*madaram baraya ma ghezaa dad*)." These words were really hard for me, so I got mental problems due to these problems and shocks that I received from the wars.

Even her mother-in-law turned against her: "My mother-in law was so aggressive towards me; she was fighting with me and saying very bad words without any reason. Anyway, she died, and God bless her." Her usage of active tense (being aggressive, fighting, and saying) shows how the pain of violence does not fall into oblivion. This incident illustrates the way in which violence becomes woven into lifelike tentacles (Das 2007).[6]

Amina has made a life in the spaces of devastation. She embodies it and inhabits it with her three children. It assumes the dimension of affect expressed through the medium of food:[7]

> We normally eat potato, *sholla* (lentils and soft rice), pasta, and some cheap vegetables. We don't want to spend more money for our food or drinks because we don't have enough income, and also we have to collect money for other expenses, like clothes and school supplies for my children. We *used to* eat good meals, such as meat, rice, *qabili* (meat with basmati rice) soup, and also we had good breakfasts like butter, cake, milk, or cookies. (Original emphasis)

Although the family has settled for less and is surviving on a day-to-day basis, Amina does not forget life in the pre-war years. Her remembrance is not a mere recall of the past (*gozashta*). My reading suggests a twofold interpretation: first, the quotidian realities are politicized. Even if one were to make a "simple" statement such as "my bread is stale," it implicates society. This is because it is structural barriers that prevent one from having access to the basic necessities of life – necessities that include issues of sociality and self-dignity. Amina's struggles are a result of, in her words, "the wars in Afghanistan." Second, her lived memory within the spaces of devastation speaks to the collective experiences of all Afghans:[8] "The wars were a very bad shock to every Afghan person." Her testimonial account ensures that the suffering and subjectivities of the people of Afghanistan are not forgotten as is currently the case. Daulatzai (2006), for example, provides a trenchant critique of the non-acknowledgment of the lives of the Afghan people forced to fight the wars of the superpowers over the past three decades.

It took several visits and conversations before I was able to understand how actively Amina was engaged in memory work, as were other women that I talked to and observed in the context of their everyday lives. Every aspect of her life – going to school, taking care of her children, her health, the rhythm of her everyday life, her relationships with kith and kin, and her widowhood – was envisioned in relation to the past, not in the form of nostalgia but as "events" rooted in her lived reality. It is this reality that gives Amina the "authority" to speak for the people of Afghanistan. Further, it is this reality that compelled her to render her narrative into a testimonial for the people of Afghanistan. Waterson

(2007) names this compulsion "a moral drive": "The drive not to allow the forgetting of traumatic events or past injustices is essentially a moral drive which seeks to comprehend the past in order to shape the future ... Essentially, this moral engagement is the reason why we are constantly revisiting and reanalyzing the past in order to understand it in the light of our present concerns" (70). Consider the following example.

Amina is aware of her vulnerability as a widow. Rather than providing a one-dimensional account of how she lost her husband, she highlights multiple factors:[9]

> I have received so many bad effects from the wars in Afghanistan through the Taliban, the Russians, and Hazara people's war [the "civil war"]. I have lost my house, my husband, my job, garden, and everything. The wars made me a widow. I have bad memories from the war, and my mother-in-law. After my husband died, I and my children passed a very difficult time. Bombs and rockets were coming back to back, and my children were crying a lot. I had no money to go to Pakistan or Iran. Finally, we lost everything and nothing was left for me except my children. I thank God (*suhran lilah*) that at least my children are alive.

By describing her struggles, her strength, her successes, and her family's survival, Amina reverses the homogenized and cultural construction of widowhood, formerly understood as someone who was socially dependent and helpless. This is a significant move in light of the fact that "homogenization slips all too easily into the exoticization of the Other, often tinged with an ethnocentric kind of pity for the oppressed condition that reads in a manner similar to colonial texts proclaiming the need to save the oppressed from themselves" (Ayotte and Husain 2005, 114; cf. Mani 1998). Amina might just as well be aware of this observation and could have "read" Daulatzai's ethnographic work on the widow's bakery project in Kabul. Daulatzai (2007) argues that it is important to understand how "gender has been inflected by violence, war and occupation and subsequently what work war and its accompanying forces have performed on social institutions, family structures and individual subjectivities in Afghanistan" (296). A focus on narrow and culturally deterministic categories such as widowhood submerges the lived impact of violence, experienced in the inner recesses of life – a space where it is rendered invisible. Alternative modes of expressions that vulnerable people resort to require our attention. Memory work is one such mode. Through her testimony, Amina complicates our understanding of widowhood as merely someone who needs to be saved; she calls on the reader to remember a politicized script – "the wars made me a widow" (*ba khatir jang showharam ra az dast dadum*). This is a significant move as war widows, in the words of one woman, are mothers and "fathers" too. Pointing to some of the children playing in the yard, she observed, "See all these children lost their fathers in war. Their mothers have raised them, educated them, given them Afghan values and will also arrange their marriages." When I inquired how they can accomplish so much, she added, "We have strength and we work hard. We keep our [extended] families together, and this is what makes a difference. We know that we are not alone. We help each other." Amina did not talk about her family except to state that she was well connected to her mother, her two sisters, her brother, and a maternal uncle.

Day comes, night ends, but for me is always night (*shab mesha roz mesha wali balai man hamesha sha ast*).

– Hamida

Hamida began her story at four o'clock on an afternoon a few days after a bomb blast (*infijar bamb*) near the Indian embassy claimed the lives of twelve civilians. This incident set the tone of her narrative: "We have lived with violence for a long time and this is our present reality." Her usage of "we" and "our" confirms a testimonial sharing of her experiences. One person captures the stories of the others while maintaining individual colours in the tapestry of life.

Hamida presented a layered account. She recounted the loss of her house that her husband, Ahmed, had built over the years for their family of five children. Frequent bombings during the civil war compelled them to leave for Iran. There, life was harsh: "We worked on the streets and cleaned Iranian homes." The family moved back and forth between the two countries: "Some months in Iran and some months in Afghanistan because my husband wanted to stay in Afghanistan even if there were wars here." This form of splintered life for eight years came to an end when Hamid Karzai became president in 2002, and the family was forcefully repatriated by the Iranian government.[10] The homeland that Hamida and her family returned to was nothing more than a devastated space: "We had no house and nothing." The director of the school took advantage of their vulnerable position. She hired them as cheap labour. Hamida worked as a cleaner and Ahmed as a gatekeeper.

The director offered them a roof and a low salary of Afs3,000 for both. Hamida said:

> We accepted this because we were in a very poor situation. I do all the chores at school including personal work of the director: washing clothes, cooking, preparing tea, cleaning her house, and looking after her children. The director is very aggressive towards us and I don't know why.

The family's one-room "house" is wet and dark; there is no kitchen or toilet. Through her everyday routine she reconstitutes the space of devastation. She wakes up at 5:00 a.m. and begins her day with ablution (ritual washing) using cold water; she then says her prayers (*namaz*). Breakfast consists of Afghan bread (naan) and tea prepared on a charcoal stove placed in a corner. When the family is up, she folds the sleeping mattresses and blankets and piles them neatly on one side. She then leaves for work. Her sixteen-year-old daughter cooks rice and vegetables for lunch and dinner. Occasionally, she adds beans when the family has spare money.[11]

Not having adequate meals, having to work long hours, and having to live in a dingy and cramped space constitute an extreme form of suffering. But this has not reached an end point. Commenting on the cumulative effects of war, including "America's war," Hamida presents her family's situation. Her elder son ran away from home: "We tried everything but couldn't find him." Her second son has become addicted: "He puts gasoline on his scarf and breathes it all day and night. I have asked him many times for the reason why he is doing that, but he says nothing to me, and I am really about to go crazy." Furthermore, she says, her daughter:

> got a very serious shock and it directly affected her mind. She was about to go mad, but that time we had nothing and no money for her treatment. My mother and brothers helped me with some money, and then we took her to a doctor. Now she feels better, but sometimes the shock comes back to her, and she looks pale and has dry lips.
>
> I got asthma, and I am still facing this asthma problem. Whenever it makes me very tired, I go to the doctor who is close to our house. The doctor is from Iran. He is very kind and knows my situation. Therefore, whenever I go to him he does my check-up and pays for my medicine. In the case of any small illnesses like a headache, cold, or flu, we buy some medicine if

we have money. If not, then we do nothing and we wait until the pain goes away by itself.[12]

The exploitation at the hands of the school director bothers Hamida: "If I ask for more salary, she shouts at me and says, 'If I hear it next time, you will be kicked off from school and there will be no place [house/ room] for you to stay.'" She added, "Because of these problems, I suffer and tolerate lots of things at school and her behaviour with us. My life has so many problems and difficulties." She summarizes her own situation, "Day comes, night ends, but for me is always night because of my two sons."

These are not unlike the situations of other women, but for Hamida there are rays of light that give her hope. She counts on the education (*talim*) of her children for a better future. She observed that her husband wanted the children to work; he is tired of earning a meagre salary, but she insists that her children get an education:

> My children (*atfaal*) are partly educated as their education is not yet finished and it is ongoing. I am really interested in the education of my children, but my husband doesn't like them go to school. He says, "They should work and get money, for the time being education is not important; they should leave school and work." But I don't let him do this to my children because I know the importance of education, especially English and computers. If you know English and computers, you can find a good paying job; if not, then you will have a bad situation and life. We know that everything is in the hands of the great God, but we have to try, work hard, and get an education to have a good life (*zindagi khob*) and bright future (*ayenda dorokhshan*).

Hamida is well aware of the source of her suffering, saying, "We were healthy and fine, but during the Taliban and Americans' war, we lost everything including health." Note how she connects what are considered to be separate realms. The United States attacked the Taliban, deploying the socially constructed discourse of the "uncivilized them" versus the "civilized us." As Lindisfarne (2008) has expressed it, "The citizens of Afghanistan are repeatedly spoken of as primitive, tribal people whose barbarism is evident in their oppression of women" (28).

Both Amina and Hamida reveal the workings of the violence of war in the inner recesses of their everyday lives. They come from different walks of life. Amina is a professional, while Hamida has no formal education and cannot read or write. Yet, their suffering is not substantially different. Amina is filled with anxiety about the education of her children. To reiterate, she remembers the time when her children were hungry ("Mom, give us food") and asking for a pair of warm shoes ("Mom, it is difficult to go to school in the cold"). She worries about not having money for medicine if she or her children fall sick. This concern is linked with the time when she did not have money to bury her husband. She worries that her children do not eat nutritious food (meat and fruit that she cannot afford) and, therefore, will not have energy to study. She feels the strain of having to raise the children on her own. Her social network, she states, is thin because "some of my family was killed in the war. My father and brother are dead." Other family members have migrated or live far away: "I do not have as much contact as I used to. They are also struggling." The memory of the past experiences is fresh as she continues to struggle. The violence of war persists in a situation where she feels alone and without support.

Hamida also lives with the pain of violence. She is compelled to work in an exploitative situation. She is keenly aware of the vicious cycle: "If I and Ahmed did not work, we would not have this house. But this is not a house. It is a dark room. If I did not have this room, where would we sleep and where would we eat?" Her narrative brings to light generational remembering and silent protest. Her elder son has left home and is missing. His absence speaks of violence within the core of family life. Her second son's "escape" through sniffing gas is also a silent protest against inadequate shelter and lack of food – basic necessities of life. Her daughter embodies the trauma of war (mental health). Hamida is not alone in remembering the effects of violence on her life. Her children embody the scars of war. Memory work does not permit closure insofar as suffering persists.

Human suffering on the scale brought about by war and violence requires a societal response that could mitigate one's pain. But this does not happen. Survivors of violence find themselves isolated and alone; they are expected to pick up the pieces and move on in the wake of harsh circumstances. Testimonial memories, then, denounce a violent past while at the same time revealing its complex entanglement in the present. Those who testify seek to engage a listening audience in a situation where the world does not want to remember for political reasons, and does not make a concerted effort to understand the pain of the others. It is in this light that we can understand Hamida's comment: "In the case of any small illnesses like a headache, cold, or flu, we buy some medicine if we have money. If not, then we do nothing and we wait until the pain goes away by itself."

Making a case for political anthropology, Fassin, citing Feldman (1994, 410), observes that in "late capitalist modernity, the quantitative and qualitative dissemination of objectification increases the social capacity to inflict pain upon the Other, and ... to render the Other's pain inadmissible to public discourse and culture" (2007, xii). Amina and Hamida understand this too well. They position themselves socially and politically so that they may be heard. Allow me to elaborate on this point in the context that looms large in the violence of war: every day and life.

Every Day and Life

Amina's and Hamida's everyday lives are shaped within spaces of devastation: two bedrooms in a battered home, and one bedroom without toilet and kitchen in an "empty" space, respectively. The "broken" condition of the once-intact homes reflects a disrupted social order. Afghanistan's infrastructure of governance, health, education, and social services has yet to be built. It is in this world of lack that both women work for low wages and attempt to rebuild their lives. Through memory work (the past embedded in the inner recesses of the present), both women seek to engage a listening community. They convey the message that their lives are not unique or exceptional. Other Afghans live through similar experiences. Testimonial memories capture a collective situation, as noted earlier. They encapsulate structural violence. Amina's comments, "I had a complete life with everything" and "we have lost everything," remind us of the extent of her loss and devastation. Hamida's exploitation by the school director is a function of her structural vulnerability: there were no services in place for repatriated Afghans. The international community has taken no notice of their suffering, as Daulatzai (2006, 2008) and Khan (2008) have observed. The conditions of the battered homes are embodied in the form of "mental health" (the malaise of the body politic). Hamida has a difficult time as the social malaise has also affected her children, making her life unbearable: her days (light) have turned into nights (darkness). Reoccupation of the spaces of devastation is also a means of survival through hope. Both the women count on the education of their children for a better future. Their everyday worlds serve to critique society as much as they are sites for the remaking of life.

Das (2007) observes that the resumption of every day and life follow-ing devastation requires the availability of bare necessities that I con-textualize in relation to a series of questions: Does one have a roof over one's head? Does a family have enough to eat and sustain itself? Do peo-ple have opportunities to engage in meaningful work? Can the children attend school? Are they in a position to play and enjoy their childhood? Can one walk the streets without fear of violence? Does one have access to health care? Can one celebrate life cycle rituals and festivities? Is one able to sustain spiritual life? Can one live a life of dignity? These ques-tions are pertinent to the lives of the narrators. The issues raised have yet to be realized structurally and in a sustained way. Both the women have taken the first steps. In the midst of devastation they have resumed their everyday lives. This resumption symbolizes a larger scenario: "Af-ghanistan remembers" – despite political amnesia on the part of the in-ternational community. Consider their activities. They pray even if they have to use cold water for ablution. They ensure that their families have food despite being undernourished. They struggle to ensure that their children have uniforms and school supplies at the cost of not seeking medical help. They struggle with mental health and trauma, and yet, they present themselves as competent mothers and employees. Their ev-eryday activities form part of the rhythm of life where the memories of war are forever present (losses, dispossessions, but also reconstruction of a precarious life). They envision a future in terms of the loss of one gen-eration (they feel that their lives are "finished" in the words of Hamida) and in terms of the hope of a second generation (their children). Their courage to live in the ruins of active memories could draw the attention of the reader/larger audience.

The women have reconfigured their identities. Amina does not pres-ent herself as a widow (*bewa*) as imagined by the international aid com-munity. Her role as a mother, a wage worker, a citizen, and also an activist (discursively) can be appreciated in the light of the following observa-tion: "[The] figure of the war-destitute dependent and subjugated widow has emerged as the paradigmatic object of intervention for the many international agencies that currently work in Afghanistan" (Daulatzai 2006, 298; also refer to Stabile and Kumar 2005). It is through her ev-eryday struggles that Amina offers the following insight: "The most risky and unsafe country is Afghanistan." Commenting on the waged work of women, she focuses on the benefits: "first, they can financially help their husbands; second, they can be aware of different things happening in the world; third, they will be more involved in society and social affairs, as well as they can be good mothers for their children." Note how she maximizes a situation where some women do not have a choice but to work for wages. The point that requires emphasis is that she speaks from experiential knowledge of the violence of war. This gives her the moral authority to comment on broader issues.

Hamida foregrounds her role as a mother. She bears witness to the effects of structural violence on her children. This form of violence, experienced at the core of her being and family life, positions her to give a politicized meaning to her story. Related straight from the heart, it has poignancy and depth. She embodies history in the flesh, revealed in the pain that she experiences every day because of the "loss" of her children (one disappeared, one addicted, one with mental effects). Through her, and through the bodies of her children, Afghanistan remembers. The world must not forget.

Remembering to Write a Different Story

Acts of violence in war contain an underlying theme that is all too familiar. Wars destroy lives, undermine livelihoods, cause immense suffering, and subject the affected population to displacement and dispossession. Skirting around these issues does not capture the full scale of suffering, as Das and Kleinman (2001), Ross (2003), and Nordstrom (2007), among others, have argued. Fassin (2007) puts it this way: "Generalities of bodies – dead, wounded, starving, diseased, and homeless – as the media allow us to apprehend the global disorder, whether through war, famine, epidemic or disaster, depersonalize the others undergoing these events, including them physically in our world while excluding them morally" (xii). The women in this study have an intuitive understanding of this observation, as they made repeated references to how their lives have been dismissed and how their suffering has not been acknowledged. Recognizing the power of collective/testimonial narratives, the women have taken it upon themselves to remember their individual stories, knowing full well their contribution in bringing into relief a collective picture for the world at large: "It is not only us [my family] that have suffered. Everyone has suffered" (Nayla).

Keeping in mind that Amina's and Hamida's stories, although individualized, are part of a collective recall, I present testimonial narratives of other women to glean the formation of the larger tapestry with different colours, fabric, and motifs. I have not sought to present a homogenized picture. Variations reveal compelling nuances.

Effects of War: A Personal Story

Fatima began her testimony around 11 a.m. Her immediate audience consisted of me, her daughter, and two of her neighbours who had come by out of curiosity about my visit. As Fatima relayed her story, she continued cutting the vegetables for the midday meal. Acknowledging other women's presence, she stated, "What I have to say is something that we have all experienced. My story is not that different from theirs." It is on this larger note that she gave the following account:

> There are so many wars [Taliban, Americans, Russians, and mujahideen] that have had a bad effect on us. We lost everything including house, mind, clothes, health, and possessions. At that time, we were living in Karte 3-Kabul [district]. It was during the time of the civil war that a rocket was thrown into our yard. My little sister was playing around in the yard. She died due to this rocket. We got a very big shock, and even I am still not feeling healthy and relaxed in my mind. After that accident, we went to another area for three years. We rented a house and my father was paying the rent. The area was filled with Hazara [ethnic group] people. Once, when my father was going somewhere, Hazara people took him to their place. He was detained for one week. We heard [after that] that he had been killed by the Hazara. During this one week we were looking around and searching for him. We never found his body. Finally, we lost everything and were left with so many health and mental problems without [my] father. I had to get married so that I would not be a burden on my family.

Fatima's recall of violence is not passive in the way of mere reflections on the past. She names the places (the yard, the district where they lived, and the road where her father was kidnapped) to show how violence entered into her family's lived spaces. She places the events in time: "it was during the civil war." She mentions other wars, alluding to the full spectrum of conflict and violence that remains unnamed, as noted earlier. Fatima also projects the event into the present. Her mother died from shock, and she was compelled to marry before she was ready. Both events affect her deeply. She embodies the tragedies that have befallen her family. It is through the temporal and spatial grounding of these events that she captures the imagination of the audience. This is what constitutes memory work. Fatima seems to have an intuitive understanding that any matter-of-fact mentioning of the loss of her sister and father would render them each into simply numbers without names. This is why she needs to remember.

Violence at the Border

The memory work of other women is specific to their circumstances, but does not differ in terms of shared experiences. It is this fusing of personalized accounts into the history of their country that gives memory its poignancy. Samira's account is compelling in that it does not involve physical violence. She is displaced in ways that are not easily noticeable:

> My life was good, and we had a middle condition [that was] not so high [but] not so bad. We had a house, lands, garden, and everything. But when I got married, my husband had a very low economy. His family was lower than my family. At that time, my husband was a porter and still he is a porter. I did not accept to marry him, but my family insisted that I accept this man because they wanted to go to Australia as my brother was there. My family said, "Your brother can only invite four to five family members. It is not possible to take you there. Also we cannot leave you alone. So it would be good to get married so that we don't have to worry about you." Then I finally got to marry that man. My family lost their house, garden, and land during the wars. This is the reason why they had to move.
>
> I had a good life in my father's house, but not with my husband. As you know, that porter job [brings in] very little income. He is also selling plastic toys from a handcart in the bazaar, so sometimes he gets Afs100, sometimes Afs50, and sometimes nothing. This is not enough for my children's school supplies. We have daily expenses like clothes, food, and fuel.

Samira sacrificed for her family's well-being, a sacrifice not limited to a one-time event. Her marriage into a poor family means ongoing struggles. There were structural factors at work: her family's displacement, the border-crossing regulations, and the cultural norm of marrying off daughters rendered her vulnerable. Of notable interest is her active recounting of her and her family's *majburi* (helplessness). She, too, embodies the past in the present. She remembers because she has to live with the violence of poverty. If she had been allowed to cross the border with her family, her story would have been different.

Resumption of Life: Ambiguities and Tradeoffs

Other women testified in terms of enduring losses. Leila, for example, related how her right hand was permanently injured by a rocket when she was baking naan (Afghan bread) in the *tandor* (clay oven) in her yard: "To this day, I cannot do much work with my right hand." To prevent further attacks, the family had to move to another district and was, thus, internally displaced.

Razia noted, "I have bad and sad memories of war, and I will not forget those days. Especially, I lost my husband during the Taliban regime in a bombing." She then talked about her struggles of having to raise her children on her own, giving examples of survival and also recovery. She noted how she bought a pair of shoes for her son minimizing one week's food budget. She also borrowed money so that her daughter could have a lunch box "that she had been wanting for months." Her eldest son (aged twelve) went to work so that her other three children (aged seven, nine, and ten) could attend school. These are small steps that speak to the resumption of life, however shattered it may be – a condition brought about in the wake of violence and devastation.

Occupying In-between Spaces of Loss and Recovery

"How do we live like a family when that which defines family life no longer exists?" (Nordstrom 2007, 249). Noting that "family is a historical continuum and home the place where it unfolds," Nordstrom argues that its disruption can affect one's sense of self in time, place, and space (249). It is this sense of self that compels people to create a world that is meaningful and livable. I argue that memory work may also be placed in between the spaces of devastation (loss) and recovery, and that it is at this juncture that violence can become knowable. How else can we understand sixty-five-year-old Ama's comment about the "shocking pain around my body" and "the big pack of medicine that I use three times a day"? These are her embodied experiences of loss and dispossession. Yet, Ama gets up at 4:00 a.m., says her *namaz* (prayers), prepares breakfast for her grandchildren, helps her daughter-in-law clean the house, brings water from the pump, and cooks occasionally. Her work falls within the realm of what we consider to be activities of everyday life except that it is embedded in pain. Ama's act of remembrance reveals the way in which her life has been shattered (she is a war widow, and the family's house and farm were destroyed). In the light of other women's narratives,

Ama's memory of pain along with recovery constitutes part of "a group memory that does not exist by itself but lives through the whole, made up of these memories that are at the same time unique and interdependent" (Debouzy 1986, 270–1; cf. Sugiman 2004, 372).

Narrative Fragments: Struggle against Forgetting[13]

The women in my study related how they never came to know their birthplace because they had to flee the Soviet invasion, and how the "civil war" rendered their families helpless (*majbur*). Consequently, some of them married early to older men because of destitution. And now, as one woman stated, she has a husband who is old and cannot work: "Now I have to work in the house, and also earn money."

The narrative fragments encapsulate the originary moments of violence embedded in everyday life. The women's recollection of the fragments is a collective endeavour – each fragment is linked to that of the other like a quilt made from different threads in time and space. The threads of the quilt comprise recollections such as: "I lost my house and now we are struggling as the rent is too high"; "I lost my husband and this is why I have to work [waged] from home and send my children to work on the streets"; "We do not have enough food and this is why I have to clean other people's homes"; "I do not have new clothes for my daughters on the occasion of Eid [religious festival], and this is why I have to do craft work which has made my eyes weak." Each woman knew the condition of the others as they conversed while they dried their clothes, collected water, washed dishes in the open space of the yard, and visited each other's homes. They were aware of their collective struggles as their memory work was directed as much to each other as to the researcher. They did not want to forget how they had arrived at a situation where their children "have to work on the streets." This form of public/neighbourhood remembrance (an active process) converts "individual ownership of memory into collective remembrance turning personal grief and mourning into a call for social responsibility" (Sugiman 2009, 201). The women's active remembrance may be viewed as a struggle against forgetting. In the words of Khadija, "nobody takes note of our everyday lives as if it does not matter that we have to go hungry at times":

As I watched Farida cook beans and rice [more rice than beans], I asked her what she made of the stories of violence of war. She stated:

Let me tell you Ghatol's story. This woman did not have a childhood. She was married when she was eleven years old as her father was poor. He "sold" her to his cousin's family, as they offered him money. The family used to beat her as she was only brought in to do all the housework. Her husband died young; he was killed by an American solider. Ghatol did not see any happiness while she was alive. When she died there, her family did not give the money to bury her. We went to an NGO and they helped us to raise funds from the neigbourhood. We each gave Afs0.20 and the NGO put in the rest. Ghatol's death was not in vain. As the neighbours came to know her story, they all felt she was one of us. She has not died. She is alive as through her, we remember our stories.

Testimonial narratives reveal. (at once personal and collective) situations not captured in official accounts. In a war-ravaged country, these narratives capture violence in the inner recesses of life. Our understanding of violence, pain, injury, and harm must come from the survivors themselves, who often resort to alternative genres of expression. Early on in my research, I identified two ways through which the women engaged in memory work: references to "before" and "after," and the recall of originary moments of violence in war. It is through these two means that memory is activated to emphasize the point that the past is present. The women have conveyed the message that they are living with the effects of violence and that these effects are not acknowledged by the outside world. In this vein, the elite stakeholders who have made Afghanistan what it is ("a wounded country") have a responsibility to set things right.

Through the testimonial mode, the women have shared their memories of lived experiences. They have spoken, and in the process, they can legitimately make a claim for acknowledgment and validation of their suffering and loss, not excluding their agency in remaking their worlds, however precarious these may be. Testimonials are not monologues, and therefore, the stories they tell have the potential to engage a listening audience. I echo Hua's observation that people who are subjected to violence "often attempt to maintain at the centre of national [international] memory what the dominant group would often like to forget" (2005, 201). Oppositional memorializing, she argues, can convert "individual ownership of memory into collective remembrance, turning personal grief and mourning into a call for social responsibility, social change and activism" (cf. Bold, Knowles, and Leach 2002, 129). Testimonial narratives, shared by the women in this study, will not have a closure insofar as their suffering is not publicly acknowledged. Hence, the act of remembering continues in the diaspora.

3
Bearing Witness

In this chapter, I present a reading of Meena's testimonial account complemented with insights from other Afghan women, all of whom reside in a low-income housing area which I refer to as Valley View, Burnaby. Engaged in the act of self-witnessing, the narrators created a space for others to witness with them a powerful mode to turn personal grief into social accountability.[1]

Research is a form of witness, and hence, it requires attentiveness on the part of the listener-reader, argues Ross (2003). This endeavour poses a dilemma for anthropologists given our close encounters with the respondents. We cannot assume that our closeness diminishes the politicized difference between us and them. To resolve this dilemma, LaCapra (1999) suggests the term *empathetic unsettlement*, "a kind of virtual experience through which one puts oneself in another's position while recognizing the difference of that position, hence not taking the other's place" (cf. Ross 2003, 4). I consider this middle-ground position to be viable for bearing witness in the diaspora where a double moment is at work: the trauma of war in the homeland and the trauma of social exclusion in the country of settlement. It is in this spirit that I share Meena's story.

The Story Must Be Witnessed

Meena migrated to Canada in 1998 with her second eldest daughter (*dokhtar*), Nasrin. Like other women in this study, she came from a secondary country, India, where she lived for seven years with her husband and five children (four daughters and a son).[2] Meena had lived through wars and civil strife in her own country. A decade of the former Soviet

Union's presence (1979–89) had rendered Afghanistan into a battle-
ground for the Cold War. The United States provided arms and am-
munition to several hundred anti-communist mujahideen (resistance
fighters) to fight a proxy war, converting Afghanistan into a landmine
(Cooley 1999; Donini et al. 2004; Dupree 2004; Goodson 2001; Hirschkind and Mahmood 2002; Khattak 2002; Rubin 1995, 2000, 2002; Saikal
2006; Stabile and Kumar 2005). During the time of the Soviet Occupation, 1.5 million Afghans lost their lives, 2.5 million were injured, and
1.1 million were internally displaced. Out of the five million refugees,
2.6 million lived in camps in Pakistan and Iran, where the living conditions were only marginally better than in war-torn Afghanistan (Brodsky
2003). This is what Meena had to say about life in her country during
this time:

> All our houses were bombed (*khanahai ma bambard shod*). Several bombs
> came [down in] our neighbourhood. I am not saying that the situation
> was bad only for us. No, it was bad for everybody in that area. When they
> bombed a neighbourhood close to us, eighteen families were killed.

She continued:

> Who cannot be happy in their own country? Who likes to be homeless and
> confused? Who? Don't you like your home country? Everybody likes to live
> in their home country so far as there is peace (*solh*), food (*ghezaa*), and
> happiness (*khoshi*).

Note how Meena engages the reader through the usage of words like
"who," "you," and "everybody." Meena's memory work takes place within
this broader social context, a politicized space as the situation depicted
applies to all, not just the individual.[3]

Meena related that her family had to flee Afghanistan to avoid the ab-
duction of her daughter by the mujahideen. Following an incident when
a bearded man came to the house at 2:00 a.m. asking for her daughter,
Meena's husband (Mohammed) sold their house at a low price and used
the money to get fake passports for India. Their eldest daughter, who
stayed in Afghanistan as an airline hostess, supported the family for a
year (1995–96) until the Taliban forbade women to work outside the
home. Meena's husband left the family in search of work, and Meena
lost regular contact with him. Meena and Nasrin were accepted into
Canada as government-sponsored refugees on the grounds that she was

a "single mother." Her other daughters got married. Upon migration, Meena sponsored her husband. The couple is still separated after five years despite the fact that the judge has accepted his application for immigration. Meena is in agony as she is separated from her husband. In response to my question on health, Meena observed:

> This [health] depends on my need for my husband (*showhar*). He needs me and I need him. He is my husband. He is depressed. All my depression is about this. My illness is about this. I have cried and cried, shouted, and screamed, but no one has listened to me.

Not a day goes by when Meena does not remember and think of Mohammed. His framed picture hangs on the wall. On one occasion when she served tea and cookies, she noted, "I always keep these in the house. They are my husband's favourite. Whenever a guest came to the house, he would say, 'Serve them the cookies.'" Every time I talked to her, his name came up in the conversation. She misses him a lot. She worries, as he is not keeping very well. Two frameworks serve to capture her agony along with her own process of settlement in a new country: the language of everyday life and remembering through one's wounds.

Speaking through the Language of Everyday Life (*Zindagi Rozmara*)

Feminists have endeavoured to document the everyday lives of women, in order to highlight two issues. First, women's everyday activities have been rendered invisible for the benefit of the capitalist system. Without their unpaid work within the private sphere and low-paid work in the market-based system, the market system would be less profitable (Smith 1987). The gendering of everyday life is, therefore, of interest as it reveals the workings of the larger system in a localized space. Second, women's engagement with the materiality of everyday spaces has brought into relief numerous ways in which they subvert the system – an aspect that is critically important as it contains the seeds of social change (Das and Kleinman 2001; Das 2007; Dossa 2005).

Everyday life, then, featured high on our interview schedule. Meena is a busy woman. Our conversations were often interrupted by the needs of her two-year-old granddaughter. She would comment, "If only my husband were here, he could play with her. It would make him happy; he has gone through so much in life." She remembered the day when he left in search of work in India: "He only took two pairs of trousers and three shirts ... I cannot live without him." Meena also cooks for the family (her daughter and her son-in-law) and does all the cleaning: "My daughter is working. She has long days. When she comes home she has to take care of the baby." In her account, Meena highlights the script of grandparenting without pay so that the younger members of her household can undertake waged work. But she does not focus on the work she does in the house that would reveal the unrecognized linkage between the public and the private. Meena's everyday life is filled with one worry: that of her separation from her husband:

mental health

> I have become ill (*maris budan*). I have got [high] blood sugar. I am sick because of my stress for my husband. In any case, he is my husband. We lived together. He is in India [and] is sick as well. He is worried, [and under] lots of pressure. I went to my doctor. She wrote a letter [for the immigration office] that I am sick. I am worried. I long for my husband and I am sad. I gave them [immigration officials] the letter. I have [problems with] depression. [The] doctor said so twice. We have sent them the letters, but I do not know why nothing happens.

Meena stated that they have taken all of the necessary steps to facilitate her husband's immigration to Canada. She has paid the government loan she received for her air ticket to Canada, she has obtained a letter of employment for Mohammed from an Iranian shopkeeper, and she has submitted all the necessary documents. The latter includes a medical certificate attesting to the fact that spousal separation has made Meena sick. The only response she has gotten from the immigration office over the past five years is: "Today, tomorrow, today, tomorrow, so we do not know when he will come."

Attending to her wounds (*zakham*) has become part of Meena's everyday routine. The term "wounds" is of value as it blurs the boundary between Meena's diagnosed illnesses (high blood pressure and diabetes) and her pain and suffering caused by over three decades of war and violence in her home country. She speaks from her wounds when she says, "I have become ill. I have got high blood sugar. I am sick because of my stress for my husband." Her illness, then, cannot be reduced to clinical diagnoses where the sociopolitical context remains buried. She is on medication, which means that the onus is on the individual to get well. Societal institutions are, therefore, absolved from responsibility (Lock and Kaufert 1998).

Meena is not the only one who remembers through her wounds on a day-to-day basis. Consider the following two scenarios, relayed by Raqib and Salima, respectively:

I was at home once. We had made some food. I told my son to go to the bazaar and buy something. He left, and I went to wash my hair. I had washed all the clothes and cleaned the house [when] a boy from the neighbourhood came and said, "Lady, your son was taken from the road. They put him in a car and left." I put on my burqa, and ran to the streets. I did not know where to go. The car had stopped somewhere close by to get other boys, ten to eleven years old. So, I found the car and told that man: "Dear father, please. I will go on my knees [to beg you], but do not take my son." He said: "No. We have to." And I have seen so many things. Our sons and children are beaten and slashed on the streets. So much cruelty we have seen. No one can believe.

The import of this memory is highlighted by the disruption of what we regard as everyday activities: cooking (mother), and going to the bazaar for a missing ingredient (son). It shows how war and violence enter civil spaces, the end result of which is drastic displacement of people and loss of lives. Although Raqib's son returned, it did not lessen her trauma as she remembers his friends being "beaten and slashed on the streets."

After Raqib finished her story, Salima stated:

God knows that we have seen the killings of people, our neighbours, other people and relatives. Seen them dying. I have suffered so much. Still, when I see someone without a leg, I suffer for that person. But what should we do? Go where?

Every woman in my study had multiple stories (*qesa haa*) that they remembered on a daily basis for the simple reason that their wounds have not healed in their new country of settlement, Canada. Neglect and institutional insensitivity to their pain and suffering have given rise to more wounds, now embedded in the bodies of the women. Here, the issue is not that of the system itself, but the non-recognition of violence in the inner recesses of life. There does not seem to be a vocabulary that captures the enduring pain within this space. The narrators have taken it upon themselves to remember the multiple ways in which violence is entrenched in everyday life. How would we explain Rahima's pain when stating that her father, brother, and sister passed away in the Taliban bomb blasts? Her mother died from shock, but not without taking a promise from her that she would take care of her traumatized younger brother. To this day, Rahima has not married: "I promised my mother, and the only way I can take care of my brother is not to marry. If he marries, I will marry, but it will be too late for me to have children." How do we account for this double loss: deaths and self-sacrifice? These memorialized stories need to be heard politically.

It is important to note that the survivors take on the role of self-witnessing where the memory of pain is intertwined with attempts at recovery. Meena, for example, began taking walks and visits the library, as she loves reading. She also went to Surrey (25 km from her home) by bus to explore the city. Being a kindergarten teacher in Afghanistan, Meena wanted to babysit other children for pay. The extra money would help her with household expenses, including her medication. But she is scared to do this job. Her social worker informed her that if she dropped the baby, owing to her dizzy spells, she would be sued. Legalities trump subjectivities and personhood.

Other activities that form part of women's routine include going to a makeshift mosque on Fridays, participating in Afghan women's drop-in programs, and keeping in touch with relatives in other parts of the world. But these activities may be considered "peripheral" as each narrator's pain and suffering are still fresh. In the words of Nahila, "The wounds have not healed." Below are two accounts, from Meena and Nargis, respectively:

They took everything from us. Everything was destroyed, even our homes were bombed. Three or four times we had bombs [come down on] our house. For a minute, all our houses were shaking. Mirrors got broken and shattered glass came like rain on our head. Blood everywhere, and people were dripping in blood because of all those ruins. So we had [a] very bad situation in Afghanistan. Many people lost their legs, hands, and other body parts.

Nargis stated:

No electricity, no lamp, nothing. You cannot see. You are scared. All the noise, all the bombs were over our heads. So, I had also illness at the time. My legs did hurt. So we had so much misery. We had no choice but to leave the country, leaving everything behind: our house, furniture, rugs, china, and our lives there [meaning way of life].

Stories of suffering can be pathologized. Kleinman and Kleinman (1997, 10) make two points. First, experiences of violence can be turned into "trauma stories" by institutions that deal with asylum seekers. Second, in the hands of medical professionals, these memories/real life events are converted into images of victimization – a dehumanizing stance. Based on these observations, these authors pose the question: "We need to ask, however, what kind of cultural process underpins the transformation of a victim of violence to someone with pathology?" (23). For these authors, a step forward includes ensuring that local participants and stakeholders are included in the process of policy making and the development of programs. Beyond policy, I would argue, they need to engage in memory work – *history in the flesh*, to use Fassin's (2007) term. The essential first step is to recognize the violation of everyday life.

This goal cannot be fully accomplished without listening closely to what the participants have to say about their experiences of suffering and pain. And the listening is not merely confined to words. This does not mean that we should underestimate the power of words. The women in my study made good use of words to portray memory images: "shattered glass," "dripping in blood," "missing legs and hands," "grief in my body," and many others. But we must also acknowledge that words do not fully capture violence. Furthermore, words and stories of marginalized people are not valorized unless they resonate with the language of the dominant group. Collins (2000) puts it this way: "Oppressed groups are frequently placed in the situation of being listened to only if we frame our ideas in the language that is familiar to and comfortable for a dominant group. This requirement often changes the meaning of our ideas and works to elevate the ideas of dominant groups" (vii).

To avoid the situation of diluting their experiences of suffering, or risk the possibility of having them appropriated by institutions, the women in this study took on the stance of wounded storytellers – a position that allowed them to witness their own stories (Dossa 2004; Frank 2000; Ross 2003). It is at this level that the women sought to engage the reader/ researcher so as to effect multilayered changes ranging from small acts to large-scale solutions. The emphasis is not on the expert (anthropologist or health and service provider) assuming the position of a witness – a top-down approach – but on ethical listening with a bent towards *speaking and remembering with* our research participants and *not for them*. The goal is to let the participants represent their own worlds inasmuch as this can be made possible in an ethnographic setting. It is in this vein that we can explore stories from the wounds.

The Wounded Storytellers: "Afghanistan Has Been Destroyed"

Wounds are stories that capture experiences of pain and suffering. Rather than being individual acts of narration, the stories, notes Frank (1995; also refer to Jackson 2006), contain narrative truths suppressed by the dominant language. Stories make it possible for sufferers to position themselves as witnesses to their suffering, inviting audiences to reciprocate. This is because stories have "the seeming ability to fuse then and now, here and there, the one and the many" (Jackson 2006, 231). This is what gives the story from the wounds its power.

As Frank (1995) expresses it, "What makes an illness story good is the act of witnessing that says, implicitly or explicitly, 'I will tell you not what you want to hear but what I know to be true because I have lived it'" (63). For Frank, the reclaiming of a voice begins with the body that, in turn, creates the self which connects with people who may be motivated to effect change within their spheres of influence. It is in this context that I will focus on ethnographic moments, to show how stories from the wounds can be acts of self-witnessing and remembering.

I can talk, I am not afraid of anything.

– Meena

Meena says more than what appears on the surface. To begin with, it is an act of breaking out of structural silence, as people do not ordinarily say, "I can talk" or "I am not afraid of anything." The women in my study have been silenced not because they cannot speak, but owing to our failure to listen to the larger narrative that implicates us (the First World) in the destruction of Afghanistan.

To not see and acknowledge the painful face of Afghanistan is morally wrong, as it was the Cold War between the two superpowers, and of late it is the US-led "War on Terrorism" that has destroyed the country. The regional powers are not absolved in perpetuating violence. As client states, Pakistan, Saudi Arabia, Turkey, and Egypt have supported what Lindisfarne (2008) refers to as "the American military machine." During the time of the Soviet occupation, the United States armed and trained the jihadis (fundamentalist anti-Soviet resistance fighters). The fighters received no training in governance. As is reported on Antiwar.com (2003): "Since the time of the Soviet invasion, Afghanistan has been a country in conflict. War and strife have been a constant part of the daily life of its citizens. Yet time and again, it has not been the people of Afghanistan,

but outsiders who have been the real cause of this pain and destruction"
(also refer to Lindisfarne 2008).

Rahima expressed the situation of Afghanistan this way:

> Afghanistan has lived with killings (*qetal*) and war (*zang*) and suffering
> (*gham*). We all are homeless and kids who should be educated are homeless
> and in mountains and deserts. All of them have been involved in criminal
> roles. Today, Afghanistan is involved in so many crimes and drugs. What is
> the reason? All these countries [foreign powers] made this happen. I mean
> we in Afghanistan, we did not make the weapons. Who would put the guns
> in their hands? Someone needs to do that in order for people to fight and
> kill each other.

As noted earlier, the mujahideen and the Taliban, the two supposedly
internal regimes that brutalized the people of Afghanistan, emerged
from the US-trained military force of the jehadis. Although Taliban
members were trained in Pakistan madrasas (religious schools), they
were supported by the United States, which had taken Pakistan under its
wing (Cooley 1999). "These monsters" – the term used by the narrators –
were created by foreign powers. It is interesting that the women referred
to members of these regimes as "people with no human eyes" and "scary
faces" – indicating that they are not indigenous. Ironically, the American
War on Terrorism involves rooting out the Taliban/insurgents it helped
to create. As the United States and its allies are not able to identify particular "terrorists," they have now occupied Afghanistan for over a decade.
Several hundred civilians have lost their lives in the indiscriminate usage
of arms, including drone attacks (Johnson and Leslie 2002, 2004).[4]

The larger story that would implicate the world powers in reducing
Afghanistan to an armed camp, void of even a basic infrastructure, remains untold. Instead, the hegemonic narrative in circulation is that the
United States invaded Afghanistan to liberate its people, and especially
its women, from the cruelty of the Taliban. A second reason put forth is
that the War on Terrorism would make the world safe from terrorist attacks (Khan 2008; Khattak 2002).

It is the untold story of the destruction of Afghanistan that the women
endeavoured to narrate through their wounds. Like the Black South
African women who told their stories using socially valorized metaphors
of domesticity (Ross 2001), my research participants were aware of the
need to use alternative modes of communication that would ensure that
their stories are heard and not denigrated. Speaking as political widows,

the women in South Africa revealed their knowledge of the state's bureaucratic process, subverting the Truth and Reconciliation Commission's efforts to construct them as victims (Ross 2001, 259). Memory
work/self-witnessing, then, is one means through which an untold story
is related. To leave this task to others would mean risking strategic appropriation, by the media and the global stakeholders. Memory work
is an engaged act. When one remembers, a sensitive listener can be
drawn into the story. This process can be achieved if we live in the story,
rather than just listen to it (Frank 1995). It is in this spirit that I continue with Meena's story. It is important to note that, although each
woman focused on her own experiences, the collective story of shared
experiences remained in the forefront. For example, in referring to the
death of her husband, Nargis stated, "I was in pain, a lot of pain, but I
was not alone. Everybody lost someone, brother, sister, mother, father,
son, daughter. It was war. Everyone got killed there. People got killed in
huge numbers."

A common thread in all of the stories was the destruction of Afghanistan. Meena bemoaned the fact that it will not be in her lifetime, or even
in the lifetime of her children, that Afghanistan will be free from the
scars of war. She remembered the happy times when they lived in peace
and had a house full of visitors:

> dropping in on all occasions. Even just to say salaam (greetings). Now they
> [the United States] say there is peace in Afghanistan (angry tone of voice).
> Even if there is peace in Central Afghanistan, there is war in the four cor-
> ners of the country ... Who likes to be homeless and confused? Who? Don't
> you like your home country? (She cried.)

Afghanistan carries multiple scars, evident in the destruction of buildings, loss of lives, maimed bodies, and the dislocation of people. The
women in my study carry these scars on their bodies, and it is from this
site that they engage with memory work, individually as well as collectively. This is reflected in the work of the Revolutionary Association of
the Women of Afghanistan (RAWA). Mariam, a RAWA supporter, had
this to say:

> RAWA has felt the pain and the miseries of the people of Afghanistan, es-
> pecially its women, and that is why they can be the real representatives of
> the women of Afghanistan. I don't think that other women can be the true
> defenders of women in Afghanistan, like so many who have not spent their

life among people, who have not experienced the bitterness of the society
with their skin, bones, and flesh. (cf. Brodsky 2003, 145)

It is from the skin, bones, and flesh (wounds) that the women in my
study remember. On our part, we need to unlearn the privileged status
that we assume as experts, so that we do not dismiss the multiple ways
in which women speak and that we do not dismiss their own initiatives
to effect change, however small it may be. Here are three examples that
Meena shared with me.

Citizenship Test

I [have] dizziness. My eyes do not see well. I have done the citizenship test
twice, but I have failed. I have read, borrowed all the books for the citizenship test. I read them, but I get dizzy ... How can I do this test? I have gone
to the judge twice. They asked me questions and I answered, but then they
told me to study more. I failed. So, you know, if one is sick, nervous, and
sad, how can one not fail?

Meena's illness cannot be exclusively explained by the medical diagnoses of diabetes and high blood pressure. She relays her illness, in this
passage and throughout her narrative, in relation to grief ("There is so
much grief in my body") and sadness. Her husband's absence is making
her feel lonely and depressed, but this is not an individualized issue. In
the context of geographical breadth and historical depth, to use Farmer's (2003) words, Meena's spousal separation was caused by displacement, first to India and then to Canada.

The women in my study talked about the destruction of Afghanistan
from the time of the Soviet invasion (1979), to the present. They also included Iraq to make their point. Meena put it this way, "Now they want to
'liberate' Iraq. But look at the women and kids getting killed or disabled.
This is not liberation. Bush has destroyed the world."[5] The research participants were not content to only talk about Afghanistan. Their experiences of migration included Canada. As a settler society, and as the
long-time ally of the United States, Canada is not absolved, although
it presents itself as a kinder and gentler nation that could not possibly
engage in any kind of violence (Razack 2000).

The women undertook the task of establishing a connection between
the violence they experienced in Afghanistan and the insensitivity of the
Canadian system. Malkki (1996) informs us that refugees everywhere are

treated as the Other, a population that needs to be controlled and contained. Given our human penchant for roots, their displacement is a cause of disturbance. I would add that refugees should remind us of the havoc that the violence of colonization and imperialism has created over there – the other part of the world. But *there* is *here*, as Khan (2001) has shown. Meena's "failure" at the citizenship test implicates the society that does not see her "wounds" or remember the full story of Afghanistan, noted above.

In her account of the citizenship test, Meena provided one message: she failed the test twice owing to the fact that she is sick. But her sickness/wounds speak to a larger story. She is unable to pass the citizenship test because society has failed her on two fronts: in Afghanistan and in Canada. Meena's wounds reveal that the two are linked. *She bears the wounds of a war-torn country, and she bears the wounds of an indifferent host country.*

Wounded storytellers initiate their own process of healing, not only through the act of remembering, but also through identifying strategies that allow them to live as opposed to merely surviving. Given their vulnerable position in society – this is the reason why they are wounded – these strategies point to spaces and areas where change can be effected. They also bring into relief the fault lines of the system. It is important to take note of both aspects (loss and recovery) if we are to work towards incremental change from the grassroots level. It is in this context that I present the second example.

Scattered Spaces: Library/Clinic/Bus

When Meena discovered that there was a public library in her neighbourhood, she was overjoyed. Her love for reading drew her to this place, apart from the fact that it made her forget her sorrow and grief. Meena does not feel settled in Canada. She explained that her $400 welfare allowance is barely enough, especially when she has to pay for medical bills not covered by her basic plan, and for the special diet that she requires in order to manage her health. The fact that no one has addressed the issue of her separation from her spouse has caused her to be more ill as she grieves for her husband.

On one occasion, when Meena was walking to the library, she met an Afghan woman who advised her not to go there as she may contract SARS. The woman told her that the librarian had advised her to keep away from crowds because of her age. In the eyes of the librarian, this woman looked seventy, as did fifty-eight-year-old Meena. Meena stated, "So I came back [home]. Now I will not go there this Monday, but next Monday I will go to the library for sure."

Meena and her friend were considered old and, therefore, vulnerable to a communicable disease, SARS. Their social vulnerability and the fact that they looked old beyond their years did not draw much attention. The Afghan community in Valley View is not well served. Those who qualify for welfare receive a minimal allowance based on the size of the family. The services rendered are more in the form of patronizing programs (health sessions and recreation). The fact that the librarian wanted to "protect" these seemingly elderly women from biological disease, but had no insight into their lives and could do nothing to help these women alleviate their social suffering, speaks volumes to the way in which an exclusive focus on the diseased body masks and silences social pathologies. I would like to reiterate here that my critique is directed to the structural vulnerability of people on the social margins.

The library incident brings home two other points. First, Meena's neighbourhood contacts are limited to people from her own community. A superficial explanation would be that Meena does not speak English. Overlooked here, however, is the structural factor that there are minimal ESL classes available for Afghan women in Valley View. The premise at work is that these women are not breadwinners and that, therefore, any investment would not be economically productive. Such is the thinking prevalent in a market-oriented society. Second, despite Meena's "illness," (the dis-eased social body), she has taken the initiative to find a public place and engage in an activity that she enjoys. Meena's initiative must be built upon as it brings to light "a lively engagement between people and place" (Isabel Dyck, personal communication) – a building block for positive change.

Visiting a Clinic

About the doctor, the clinic is close to us. Thank God. I have learned [how to] go there by myself. I understand Hindi and I talk to the doctor in Hindi. Now I can comprehend English as well. [She looks happy.] I say "there is a [medical] problem." In the beginning, I took this or that person [Afghan] from the mall or whoever else I found on the street. The young girls in the mall, I told them, "I have a doctor's appointment." So they came with me and talked with the doctor. But now, why should I lie? I am good, [capable] and I can take care of everything by myself.

We have much to learn from Meena's resourcefulness and initiatives given the fact that she has scant resources (material and social) to draw from. It is interesting to note that she makes use of the Hindi language that she learned in a refugee camp in India. This is an aspect that health and social service providers do not easily identify with, as the system does not allow them to pay attention to the details of the everyday lives of their patients/clients. It is these details that can help to bring about the shift from focusing on the victimization of the sufferers towards recognizing their humanity. Acknowledging that Meena knows two languages (her mother tongue and Hindi), and that she has taken steps to learn English on her own without much professional help ("But now, why should I lie? I am good, and I can take care of everything by myself") should validate Meena's linguistic ability.

Of interest is the fact that Meena draws resources from the limited access she has to the people around her. But these people are Afghans. She has no access to the mainstream people in her area. There are structural factors at work here. Racialized minorities in Canada are demarcated into certain spaces where they are Othered and marginalized; this is compounded in the case of women (Agnew 1996, 2007; Bannerji 1995, 2000; Dossa 2004). Meena is no exception. Her trips to the library and the clinic speak to the spatial limitations of Afghan women in Canada.

Taking a Bus

When we first came, we lived in a hotel. An Afghan man taught us the bus to take. He used to work in the Canadian embassy in India. He was a nice man, and he knew English. He [helped us to] apply for our telephone as a co-signer. He told us [where] to go [to get what we needed], so he taught us [a lot].

She continues:

Once or twice people [will] tell you where to go. But then I tried to remember the streets, the numbers, the buses. And I kept [repeating]: here is Nanaimo, here is Metrotown. I wrote down the names and checked my notes. I told myself, one station, two station, three station [to count the stops], and I remembered where to get off the bus. I went to Surrey, once, twice. I went there to learn [and] I taught myself where to go. I went to a clinic to get [an] injection, and I learned [how to get] everywhere like this. I go to Surrey to see all those stores: [I go to] Hindi stores and Arabic stores to buy halal (lawful) meat. These are my happy days.

Meena debunks the myth surrounding "aging" immigrant/refugee women: namely, that they stay home, they are a social burden, and they do not know what to make of their lives in a foreign country as they are too old to learn (Dossa 2004). The way in which Meena has learned the bus routes, albeit from an Afghan, speaks to the initiative that women themselves take despite numerous constraints, which for Meena are her illness, the language barrier, a foreign environment, and material limitations (Meena was only able to take the bus after she got a discount that she is entitled to, like other citizens with limited income). Once again, structural marginalization is apparent as Meena only goes to areas where there are Hindi and Afghan stores. While one may be drawn to one's culture and spaces that echo the sounds and sights of the homeland, one must also question why migrants from the so-called Third World are not structurally at home in mainstream public places. The issue is not cultural; it is a function of structural factors (Anderson and Kirkham 1998).

The term *enclaves* has been used in the literature to conceptually explain the way in which racialized groups have been confined within their own communities to address the long-standing ambiguity within Canadian society. On the one hand, Canada needs the labour of non-white people, but at another level, it wants to remain Eurocentric. A way out of this ambiguity is to ensure that racialized minorities remain contained within particular spaces, a shining example of which is the Chinatown in Vancouver. As Anderson (1991) has argued, "Chinatown" was not the product of an ethnic community's desire to stay with its own kind. Instead, it is at once a geographical and a social construct (also refer to Lee 2012). Enclaves in the market sphere serve yet another purpose: they facilitate the exploitation of racialized minorities. Within particular low-paying and no-benefits labour slots, such as nurse's aides, domestic workers, and garment workers, minority labour (including women of colour) is used for the benefit of the larger society (Li 2003). A third aspect of enclaves concerns social invisibility. Certain groups of people are placed in locations where they are structurally overlooked, as was the case with the women in this study. But social marginalization does not translate into passivity. Adopting a pragmatic stance, marginalized people remake their worlds, even if this means taking small steps at a time as Meena's narrative reveals. These strategies are of value as they do not only point to elements that can lead to grassroots–level change, but they also identify the fundamental fault lines of the system. For example, how can the biomedical model with its focus on individual pathology broaden its parameters to include social and political factors (Scheper-Hughes 1992)?

Meena's narrative indicates that an ESL program would have to recognize her bilingual ability, which may require a different approach as opposed to the common assumption that immigrants only speak their mother tongue. This is an important point as immigrants' exposure to multiple languages and multiple cultures are often underplayed in Canada, a country that only recognizes two official languages (Bannerji 2000; Li 2003). Other languages are placed under the umbrella term of "heritage" (read: frozen in time, and existing within discrete and marginalized spaces).

While the women in this study sought to remake their worlds in the best way they could, they did not lose sight of the fact that they had a larger story to tell – not only for themselves, but for the people of Afghanistan. This aspect was revealed to me in the two sentences that were on the lips of all the women: "Afghanistan has been destroyed" and "Its people have been forgotten."

For the research participants, the aspect of being forgotten was carried forward to their country of settlement. The women were concerned that their basic needs were not met in Canada.[6] This was also part of the conversation over chai (tea) drop-ins that I attended. The women then took it upon themselves to remember two intertwined stories: the story of war (Afghanistan) and the story of the war's aftermath (Canada). The most challenging task was to link the two stories – a link that Canada and other Western countries do not recognize, as they have absolved themselves from the responsibilities of waging wars (the Cold War and the War on Terrorism) on the soil of Afghanistan. To compound the situation, the West has positioned itself as the saviour and the liberator of the people of Afghanistan, the most vocal form of which is gendered. For the Western media – which speak for stakeholders – Afghan women's liberation is measured in terms of whether women can move around without their burqas, considered to be the icon of their oppression. Western powers have failed to address substantive issues such as female education, the availability of work and career opportunities, and women's rights in a society (Abu-Lughod 2002).

The connection between the global North and the global South must be recognized if we are to write a different kind of history, one where the everyday realities of violence in the inner recesses of life are recognized. It is to highlight this unarticulated connection between the two countries (Afghanistan and Canada) that the women engage in the acts of witnessing and remembering. Our reciprocal engagement must then be to validate and acknowledge this connection that the women are making using the language of everyday life and the language of wounds. It is at this level that I have presented my argument on witnessing and remembering on the plane of social vulnerability. The connection between the two countries can be recognized by the fact that the women in this study occupy a vulnerable position in their homeland, owing to prolonged war, and in Canada, owing to the insensitivity of the system, noted above. To revisit Meena's words:

> I have become ill. I have got [high] blood sugar. I am sick because of my stress for my husband. In any case, he is my husband. We lived together. He is in India [and] is sick as well. He is worried, [and under] lots of pressure. I went to my doctor. She wrote a letter [for the immigration office] that I am sick. I am worried. I long for my husband and I am sad. I gave them [immigration officials] the letter. I have [problems with] depression. [The] doctor said so twice. We have sent them the letters, but I do not know why nothing happens.

Meena's husband is sick *over there* (Afghanistan/India). Meena is sick *over here* (Canada). The "sick" bodies/wounds of the husband and the wife connect the two worlds that are otherwise deemed to be separate. Their separation speaks to the injustice of dividing the world up in ways where one world (the West) presents itself as superior and the saviour of the Other, for the purpose of exploitation and control – the colonial narrative (Bannerji 2000; Said 1978).

I would suggest that it is within a framework of linkages between individual lives and the broader social and political contexts, as this is initially worked out by the research participants, that the act of witnessing and memory work can take place. In sum, the witnessing and memorialization of suffering must begin within the spaces that the participants have carved, and not in the largely textual space created by the experts.

Let us examine how Meena and other women in this study respond to the person-is-the-political paradigm considered to be the preserve of the expert.

We have noted that Meena first identified a primary concern that consumes her everyday life, and that is her separation from her husband (*showhar*). Meena is well aware of the fact that words, even in the form of a question as to why her husband is not able to join her, have evoked no response. Her long-time suffering, like that of the other women in this study, has been silenced for the primary reason that the world's acknowledgment of its involvement in the massive displacement of Afghan people would mean that it would have to take responsibility for putting their lives in order. The narrators emphasized that there is not a single family that has been spared the pain of this long drawn-out war, which they do not attribute to local factors.

The women therefore took it upon themselves to tell their stories of suffering and pain on their own terms, and this meant using other instruments of expression such as memory work embedded in the language of everyday life, and the stories from the wounds. It is within this context that Meena is able to tell a powerful and multilayered story: she implicates the foreign powers in the destruction of her country using body language (language of symptoms and suffering), and by linking this language to her native soil along the lines that Afghanistan is also a wounded body (bombs, destruction of houses, land filled with blood, land filled with landmines, land where countless bodies are buried). Through her wounds – also a means for remembering – Meena tells the story of indifference and structural violence that she encounters in her country of settlement. The wounds (*zakhm*) on her body speak of the isolation and loneliness that she experiences on a daily basis, including her struggle to meet her basic needs. The fact that she has fallen sicker after migrating to Canada speaks volumes of the linkage between her body and the body politic. Her remembering of the past as present should prompt us to acknowledge our complicity, as global bystanders, in the pain and misery that she and others are subjected to through circumstances not of their own making. It is within this space created by the participants/narrators that the act of witnessing and remembering takes place, and this is the first step towards bridging the gap between *here* (Canada) and *there* (Afghanistan). Nargis stated:

> We do not want to tell our stories unless it [can bring] about some results. But we should not let others speak for us. They [the system/welfare workers] do not understand, and maybe our education is higher than that of the welfare worker, but they give themselves the permission to treat us like we are nothing.

The women in our study have experienced suffering in their flesh and blood. They have also witnessed the ongoing destruction of Afghanistan, militarily and through structural violence, the damage of which cannot be measured as it tears the fabric of everyday life. When the women sought asylum in the First World, they encountered indifference and also structural violence related to mechanisms of power, an aspect also discussed by Boehm (2012) with reference to transnational Mexicans. The latter, she notes, "are often caught between here and there, whether as a person walking across the border, an individual in the United States yearning for 'home,' the partner of a migrant who has never been to the other side, or a child who is sent north or south by family members" (5). Such a situation then complicates our understanding of home as it can be made of parts and totalities dividing the whole into half here and half there. While migrants transcend borders, she notes, they are at the same time divided by them (147). This is also the case with Meena. She has crossed the border into Canada, but her life is half "there"/on the other side on account of her husband. She is neither here nor there. Meena feels that the onus is on her to remember not only for herself but also for her country. This is a difficult undertaking as social invisibility translates into social silencing.

People who have been subjected to political and structural violence seek other modes of communication to keep alive their stories of suffering and trauma (Das 2007; Ross 2001). The narrative data presented in this chapter revealed the language of everyday life and the language of the body to be salient. If these women have taken the initiative to witness and remember their own stories, what then is our responsibility as researchers and readers? We cannot overemphasize the point that we ourselves may not have endured suffering – we study it. This is the reason why we need to witness and remember *with* them and not *for* them, a position that can lead to appropriation of their stories of suffering.

Three themes are salient. First, migrant women (and their families) are entitled to social provision on a scale that would help them build a new life in Canada. Rather than taking the form of ad hoc measures, it must be systemic and connect with the everyday lives of women. Social entitlement is an issue brought into relief by Meena's testimonial narrative. Second, speaking as wounded storytellers, the women make a connection between *here* and *there*, implicating the West for their condition of displacement. Women's transnational connections with kin suggest the importance of social and cultural border crossing, with its potential to foster interconnections, within and beyond the nation state. It may be that the Afghan women – unrecognized and socially invisible – can suggest an alternative base for civic polity. Third, in their commitment to capturing local worlds in the context of the global, anthropologists can foster reflexive remembering in order to tell the full story, critically.

Chai with the anthropologist and her daughter Fahreen (Kabul).
Photo by Reshad Ahmed.

Extended family. Photo by Parin Dossa.

"I have a story to share" (Afghanistan). Photo by Parin Dossa.

"I have a story to share" (Canada). Photo by Parin Dossa.

Front-line guard: NGO compound surrounded by concrete and barbed-wire fence (Kabul). Photo by Parin Dossa.

Gated ("barbed wire") house, Burnaby (Canada). Photo by Fahreen Dossa.

Enactment of violence. Photo by Parin Dossa.

The future. Photo by Parin Dossa.

4

The Fire of the Hearth Will Not Be Extinguished

This chapter explores food and its interface with the memory work of women (*zanaan*) in Afghanistan. As a social phenomenon embedded in everyday life, food (*ghezaa*) reveals the impact of violence in the inner recesses of life. To illustrate this point, I focus on three ethnographic sites: the hearth, the vendor's cart, and the vegetable patch. Women's work at the hearth reveals their survival strategy of cooking with minimal ingredients in the absence of the staple diet of meat (*gosht*). Going beyond the materiality of food, the women's strategies include fostering social ties and cultural nurturance. In the course of the preparation and consumption of food, the women remember the pre-war past through which they reconstruct the present (*haal*) and envision a future (*ayenda*). This process is encapsulated in my summation of their words: "*the fire is diminished but not extinguished (aatash kam shuda wali dor nashuda)*."

From the inner space of the hearth, I move outwards into the space of the food vendors (*karachiwan*) stationed with their carts in the neighbourhoods (*hamsayagi*) where they reside. Known in their respective communities, they play a role in the provision of produce: they make it possible for women to obtain food in times of scarcity through the customary practice of lending on credit. Rather than being mere vendors, they encapsulate the scars of war made manifest by their mass presence on the streets of Kabul. Barely surviving from day to day, they represent violence in the inner recesses of life as their visible presence is rendered politically invisible. No attempts have been made to remedy their situation. The mutual recognition of shared memories of violence between the vendors and the neighbourhood families has created a bond that goes beyond the market model of transaction. Existing in between the inner space of the hearth and the outer space of the vendors, the

vegetable patch (a shadow of the kitchen garden) also reflects the violence of war. The patch captures a double moment: at one level, it helps
women to procure food and at another level it is a lived memorial of the
destruction caused by war (*jang*). A recurring phrase in women's memorialization was: "Our gardens were burned."

The three sites capture the disruption of the ordinariness of life,
revealed through food as a medium of memory work.[1] The everyday
struggle of cooking with minimal ingredients, not excluding hunger,
constitutes an enactment of violence. This struggle is normalized in a
war-torn country as is the produce cart and the vegetable patch. While
we can attempt to make violence in the inner recesses of life knowable,
the question for consideration is: How do we respond to the injury and
harm inflicted by war? And how do we incorporate participants' attempts
towards recovery (*roabadi*) even if it is in the form of molecular changes?
The larger issue is: what does it mean for "anthropological knowledge to
be responsive to suffering?" (Das 2003, 294).

Food as Performance

Taking a cue from Holtzman (2006), I consider food to be a form of
performance – embodying a movement from the private to the public.
Though considered to be an intimate activity, "food is integrally constituted through its open sharing, whether in rituals, feasts, reciprocal
exchange, or contexts in which it is bought and sold. One might consider, then, the significance of this rather unique movement between the
most intimate and the most public in fostering food's symbolic power, in
general, and in relation to memory in particular" (373). In short, food
(*ghezaa*) comprises an integrated unit where the material, symbolic, social, and cultural dimensions are given equal weight. An anthropological
perspective directs us to explore these aspects from the bottom up, in relation to the lived realities of people.[2] In the case of protracted violence,
the multifaceted nature of food is brought into sharper focus through
everyday struggles for survival. And this focus is tied to memory work
of critical importance as it is through the active interface of food and
memory work, I argue, that violence in the inner recesses of life can become knowable. Food as an everyday act of performance and memory as
a means of making the past present are each powerful tools in their own
right. Performing and remembering bring into sharper focus the enactment of everyday violence. While the violence of war unfolds on the everyday lives of the respondents, it does not exclude the process of recovery.[3]

As the women struggled to procure food, they remembered at the same time. And their acts of remembrance enhanced the sociocultural dimensions of food.

In their own words: "My children were hungry. They said 'Mom give us food.'" "We did not have sugar to put in our tea." "Many times we would only have tea and naan for dinner." "I remember a house full of people with plenty of food. Now we do not celebrate Eid [religious festival] as we cannot afford meat. Eid is like any ordinary day." "My children ask for meat [staple diet]. I keep quiet as I do not know what to say." These words provide a glimpse of how acts of violence are remembered through food. The provision, cooking, and consumption of food extend beyond the material level. When special occasions are rendered into ordinary days because one does not have the means to celebrate them, this speaks to the loss of symbolic/sacred dimensions. Violence in the inner recesses of life has two characteristics: it is normalized and it compromises one's humanity. Food is one medium through which these aspects come to light, enhanced through the complementary medium of memory work. Memory like food is a social phenomenon; remembering the past as present brings into sharper focus the injustices that one has been subjected to owing to acts of violence in war. The question that I continue to ask is: What do we do once we understand the inscription of violence in the inner recesses of life? As an anthropologist, I suggest an engagement with the recent disciplinary trend towards accountability in research. Accountability amounts to recognizing that disenfranchised persons have social and cultural lives that go beyond satiation of hunger. It is in this context that I present ethnographic material from the following three sites.

The Hearth

The Fire of the Hearth Is Diminished but Not Extinguished

"Food locates us. Discussions about place steer us homeward, and home inevitably leads to the hearth – the focus of the household" (Ray 2004, 131). My choice of the term *hearth*, as a starting point from which to link memory work with food, is informed by my interlocutors' reference to "keep the fires of the hearth burning." In other words, regardless of food scarcity, the women continue to cook, and what they prepare is not bereft of cultural and symbolic dimensions. Though a private and a domestic space, the hearth is a locus of warmth and hospitality. It is

from this site that food is cooked by women and served to family members and visitors, not discounting ritual occasions. A male informant observed that on his way home from work, the first sign he would look for
from a distance is the smoke; it gave him assurance that all was well with
his family. Indeed, an extinguished hearth is a poignant reminder of the
crisis that can erupt during times of war.

The hearth is also a site of memory. Hearth is a metaphor for home.
Associated with family and kinship ties, it captures "the everyday seemingly unmarked activities that take place within the houses, such as eating a meal or looking after the children. These activities involve women
and what I have called the process of kinship – that is feeding, hospitality, exchange, marriage, children, fostering and grandparenthood"
(Caesten 1997, 4). It is this encapsulation of sociality that makes the
hearth a powerful site of memory. While cooking on a charcoal plate or
a small stove, the women remember what they used to eat and what they
eat now: "We used to eat cheese, butter, eggs, milk, fruit, and cakes for
breakfast. Now we only have naan with tea (chai) and sometimes eggs
(*tukhm*)." The hearth (metaphorically and literally) lends itself to moments of recall. While making eggs, for example, Naseem remembered
the chickens in her yard and how she used to feed them and how she had
once run after one that had escaped. She remembered taking eggs to
her neighbour, who would, in turn, supply her family with apples and potatoes. She recalled, "Now we hardly have enough eggs. Our garden was
destroyed by the Taliban." Memory work – active recall – captures the
extent of the damage caused by violence. The poignancy of this deprivation hits home when one is no longer able to perform ordinary everyday
activities. Disruption of the rhythm of life is revealed poignantly through
the act of performance (cooking around the hearth) and remembering
(around the hearth).

Not being able to fully reconstitute one's world meaningfully and with
dignity constitutes a violation of the self and, by extension, that of the
family embedded in social networks. Food is all-encompassing. Its presence is felt everywhere. Though visible, food's analytical absence is strik-
ing (Smith and Jehlicka 2007; Rosenberger 2007). Considered to be part
of every day's routine, food is barely noticed except in times of crisis.
Allow me to present one example. During one of my visits to Rashida's
home, a neighbour dropped in with a newly born baby. She was unhappy
as she did not have the money to engage in the customary practice of dis-
tributing Afghan sweets to family and friends. Rashida observed that she

was one among many others: "If we cannot follow our tradition because of lack of resources, how else can we celebrate?" Consider a contrasting scenario. On another occasion when I was visiting Leila, an Afghan man came in his car to distribute Afghan sweets. He had become a father, and as his late mother had lived in the area (Kote Shangi), he felt that giving sweets to the children of poor families would bring him *barakat* (blessings). The three trays (60 pieces in total) were not enough. Noting that many children were left out, Leila observed, "This man has come from abroad. He has no idea how many people have become poor because of the wars." Below I explore these themes, while not overlooking the aspect of resumption of life.

In the Afghan households that I visited, cooking is gendered. It starts early in the morning, and is preceded by two activities: prayers (*namaz*), and the sweeping of the floors.

When I get up, I say *namaz*, sweep the floor, and light the fire for chai (tea).
                                                                    – Farah

My visit to the homes of the women in the districts of Khair Khana and Shash Darak took place largely in the mornings, a time that was convenient for them. By the time I arrived with Yalda, the women had said their *namaz* and had swept the floor. Sweeping the floor is of symbolic import. It connotes the beginning of a new day filled with hope and optimism. The women also swept up "the dirty material that comes from outside" (Farah). Originating from potholes, open gutters, and uncollected garbage, the debris points to the spaces of devastation. There have been times when the women have swept up debris from bomb blasts revealing that violence has not been far from their lives: "Even my mother remembers sweeping bits and pieces from bombs. She asked me 'When will the war end?' I told her, 'Let us pray that it ends soon.'" Mehrunisha's recalling reminds us of the everyday violence (*gadwadi rozmara*) that these women and their families live with. It is a form of violence that disrupts lives. A bomb blast in their area means that the children do not go to school for a couple of days until things are quieter. It also means that, for a day or two, no one goes out. This may amount to families going hungry as shopping is done on a day-to-day basis, depending on the money earned from casual work. Visiting kith and kin are curtailed after a bomb blast as travelling is considered risky. On one occasion, Mehrunisha informed me, she could not attend her brother's funeral at the other end of the town as several parts of the city had been subjected to bomb blasts. Disruption of everyday life translates into inability to carry out meaningful activities – activities that affirm our status as social beings. I consider this to be a form of violence that takes place in the inner recesses of life where it is barely noticed by the outside world. The effects are not measurable. I had several opportunities to visit the sites of bomb blasts, as they occurred frequently. Often, the attention was directed to the loss of lives and destruction of property. The question that remained unasked is the enduring impact of violence on the lives of the people.

The disruptions do not spare what the women regard as sacred: *namaz*. There are times when the women do not have water to perform ablution (the washing of the face, hands, and feet before *namaz*). In winter, they cannot use the freezing water in the absence of heating facilities. Lack of adequate space for performing (body in movement) *namaz* is also an issue as most of the women live in one- or two-bedroom homes with a family of four to six. Roshan, for example, noted that she does not have enough space to say *namaz* with her young daughter – a generational discontinuity from the point of view of experiential learning. Not being able to fully reconstitute one's world meaningfully and with dignity constitutes a violation of the self and, by extension, that of the family, as noted earlier. Below, I explore these acts of violence revealed in the preparation and consumption of food, not overlooking the aspect of resumption of life. Food is used interchangeably here with culinary performance to emphasize two points: first, it suggests an active mode embedded in memories where the presence of the past is palpable; second, the term *food* captures feminine resourcefulness.

Minimalist Food

A powerful and enduring image imprinted in my mind is that of the women cooking with minimal ingredients: seasonal and, therefore, inexpensive vegetables (*sabji*), soft rice and lentils (*sohelleh*), and beans supplemented with Afghan bread (naan). Day in and day out, my participants in the Kabul districts of Khair Khana and Shash Darak prepare what appears to be the same meal.[4] Over time, I recognized subtle variations in the texture and the taste. These variations are introduced through two sources: (1) a generational and gender-based stock of memory and (2) interdependent social ties. Having grown up in extended families, the

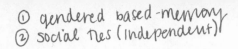
① gendered based-memory
② social Ties (independent)!

women watched their mothers and their female kin improvise during times of scarcity and deprivation. They learned that the closely related work of providing food and fostering social relationships is gendered. And they have accepted the fact that they will have to do without the staple diet of meat, an item that has become unaffordable "as its price has gone up and up and up" (Farida).

When I entered Khadija's house, she was cooking sticky rice (inexpensive compared with the superior basmati), which she planned to serve with lentils. When I asked if she makes this dish the same way every day, she replied, "No, I cook it differently. Otherwise my family will not feel that they had a proper meal." She changes the recipes as much as possible:

> One day it is plain rice with beans, another day I make it into a *palao* (a dish traditionally made of rice and meat). I cannot buy meat. It is too expensive so I use peas and carrots. Other days, I just add herbs and onions. It creates a different flavour.

She noted that on the rare occasions that she has guests (her in-laws from a rural area) for dinner, she cooks eggplant (*banjan*). She recalls the times when her mother served this dish as a substitute for meat. "My mother would laugh and say, 'here is a one-legged chicken.'" She continued: "In the past, life was hard. Now, it is harsh. Our struggles for food do not end."

Day in and day out, I observed the women preparing "different" meals with the same ingredients. I was struck by how they put together a meal working from a cramped space that was barely a kitchen: a low stool on the floor and a charcoal stove with only a few utensils. They were competent with the culinary skills that they employed under conditions that were otherwise harsh. When they washed their utensils they had to rub very hard and for a long time to remove the black stains left by the charcoal. It was only when I got to know the women that I began to realize how their status was undermined as they had lost one area that they could call their own: the hearth within the space of a fully equipped kitchen. Scarcity of food along with the absence of the staple items of meat (*gosht*) and fruit (*mewa*) also affects their ability to foster social relationships. Without a meat dish, dinner invitations are not given. By way of an illustration, I would like to present the example of meat, an item that encapsulates a way of life: lost but also reconstituted (the hearth fire is not extinguished).

The Absence of Meat (Gosht)

I often visited Tamiza since I could converse with her in Urdu, a language in which she was well versed after having lived in Pakistan for eight years. Upon her return to Afghanistan, she and her family had acquired a taste for *biryani* (spiced rice mixed with meat). This is not unusual. The places where we reside often leave their imprint on us. Many of the women I met talked about culinary adaptations from having living abroad as refugees. Some of the returnees from Pakistan had adopted the Pakistani dress of *salwar* (long pants), *khamis* (long loose shirt), and *do-pata* (long scarf). This outfit has become popular among women in Afghanistan, along with the music (the Indian Bollywood and Pakistani *kawalis*/songs).[5]

Tamiza's life as a displaced person in Pakistan was hard. Her husband had casual construction work while she and her four children, aged seven to thirteen, undertook income-generating work making pickles at home. Two of the older children attended school for half the day. She obtained milk, cheese, and yogurt from the two goats that she kept in the yard – feminine resourcefulness. After a hard day of work, the family would look forward to a hot meal "especially on the days when we had *biryani*." She described this dish as filled with *barakat* (plenty): "Even if you have little meat, you can add vegetables and potatoes. And rice is filling. And we can invite guests to join us. It is a dish that you can stretch," she mused. Since their return to Afghanistan, she does not make this dish as "my children ask for meat." She recounted: "They say, 'there is no meat' in the dish. I do not know what to say. So I do not cook it." *Biryani* extends beyond the materiality of food. In Pakistan, the family consumed it after a hard day's work. In Afghanistan, it evokes the memory of exile.

The dishes that the women missed most were *maushawa* (beans with small meatballs), *kebabs* (ground beef), and *qabili palao* (basmati rice dish with meat). The marked absence of meat in the households also compromises social life. In Afghan homes, meat is associated with sociality. "I remember a household full of people. We always had guests for dinner. On the occasion of Eid, I had new clothes and jewellery. When we visited the homes of our relatives, there was so much food. Meat was the main dish," recalled Rizwana. As an expensive item that takes time to prepare, meat symbolizes hospitality. It lends itself to the preparation of a variety of dishes, and serving different meat-based dishes is a signature of welcome.

Meals Foster Close-Knit Social Networks

Food embraces the materiality of life. At one level, it is consumed for the express purpose of nutrition and energy, but beyond that it has a social function: "Those who eat together have a heart-to-heart bonding. Those who eat separately, their hearts are separate" (*kasani ke juda khorak meku-nand, qalb hai anha ham juda ast*). This oft-repeated saying in cultures of the East captures the significant role that food plays in fostering social relationships. Having *mehman* (guests) in the house for a meal is considered to bring *barakat* (abundance). The women talked about two types of guests: visitors invited to stay for a meal because there was enough food to go around, and visitors with formal invitations. Formal get-togethers were frequent in the past: religious occasions such as Eid, Navroz (the New Year), return from a pilgrimage (hajj), and life cycle rituals were celebrated in different ways as the occasion required it and according to customary practices. One can only imagine the loss that the women experience in not being able to have *mehman* for dinner owing to a scarcity of food, or when they stated that special occasions have become "ordinary" owing to a lack of resources. These deprivations compromise one's sense of what it is like to be human – namely, a sociable and meaning-making person. Lind and Barham (2004) reinforce this point, stating that "food is woven into an understanding of what it means to be part of the human community" (53). Frema captured well the sentiments of other women: "I really like to have guests at home and invite them for a meal because a human being is social. There is a saying of Prophet Mohamed, '*mehman* is God's friend.' Therefore a Muslim must love their guests and have good relations with them and invite them for a meal if they are able to do this."

Although the get-together occasions are becoming fewer, the women keep the memories alive through improvisation – minimalist meals that speak to the absence of meat. Staple food items like meat and fruit are not forgotten. They form part of an envisioned future. On one of my visits to Frema's house, she served raisins and sunflower seeds as a snack with chai. She stated, "Next time you come, I will serve you fruit." Except for apples, which Frema's family obtains from a neighbour to whom she gives eggs, the family has not eaten fruit for close to three years. Likewise, when I visited Fatima she observed, "I cannot invite you for a meal as we cannot afford meat. When you come next time, I will serve you proper Afghan foods."

Jamila was putting away the food that she had placed on the *desterkhan* (cloth placed on the floor). She had her brother-in-law over for a meal for which purpose she had borrowed money from a neighbour. "I had to buy some meat and fruit," she said, "If in-laws are visiting, you have to make them feel welcome." And this also means inviting close relatives to one's home. Just as Jamila was about to pick up the fruit placed on the front end of the *desterkhan,* she remarked, "This is how I like my life to be like. I would like meat and fruit and a variety of dishes like in the past, but not with borrowed money. I am willing to work hard so that we can have good meals and are able to invite *mehman.*" She equates good meals with a good life, revealing the importance of food in fostering social relationships. She continued:

> If my father were alive, this is where he would have sat. This place [centre] is for him. I feel his presence. I remember his generosity. Anyone who came to the house, he would say, "You have to eat something. You cannot go unless you have something." He would make sure that there was lots of food and the guests got generous portions.[6] He died four years ago, when there was a bomb blast in our area.

The death of a person translates into everyday violence of material, social, and cultural deprivations. For example, when Mah Puri's husband died under the hands of the Taliban, her son was compelled to move to Pakistan with his family as his life was also at risk "because the Taliban did not like us, the Tajiks," she noted. He is settled there and, therefore, cannot move back to Afghanistan. "I am now old. I miss my grandchildren. My daughter did not get married to take care of me." Mah Puri says that she feels guilty that she "ruined" her daughter's life. She only has two children, and "when I die, I do not know what will happen to my daughter." Imagine the unusual situation of the grandmother living alone with an unmarried daughter owing to the social harm inflicted by violence. Were it not for the wars in Afghanistan, Mah Puri would be living a life of peace with her son and grandchildren. The wars have deprived her of the joy of being with her grandchildren.

I had to walk some distance to reach Shyrooz's house. It was located on a narrow alley in a rundown neighbourhood. On the way, I came across a small tent pitched for a temporary period. When I inquired as to whether there was an occasion, an elderly person informed me that there was going to be a dinner in honour of a Haji – the title given to a person who returns from a pilgrimage to Mecca. In response to my question as to whether her family was invited, Shyrooz said: "In the past [pre-war period], the whole family would be invited. Now it is one person from each family. My husband is the only one who will go." Gradually, I was able to put together a picture of this event. To begin with, the tent is put up by a professional to ensure that it does not collapse. The professional's charges vary from Afs50 to Afs250 depending on the size of the tent and the economic condition of the neighbourhood. He charges less in low-income neighbourhoods. The payment is made by three-to-five close-knit families who also share the food cost. I learned later from Zahra that this is a new development. "In the past, the host family would generally bear the full cost. But now it is not possible. There are so many people who are poor (gharib) because of the wars," she explained (original emphasis). In the pre-war period, gharib was a variable condition. A failure of the harvest would render one gharib at that particular period; an abundant harvest meant the reverse. The variable reality of being gharib or rich (daulatmand) meant that families assisted their kin and kith reciprocally. This scenario translated into a local support system that is no longer in existence. As Farida expressed it, "These days everybody is poor. This is why life is so hard for all of us. This is what happens in wars. We in Afghanistan have lived through so many wars. We are now tired."

Nevertheless, it is important to acknowledge the collaborative work (however reduced) of the local people in maintaining the symbolic, cultural, and social import of food – work that can best be appreciated in the light of the global food system that is making inroads into Afghanistan, evident in the increasing presence of supermarkets and imported foods. With its focus on "atomistic individualism and a culture of consumption" (Radin 1996, 83; cf. Lind and Barham 2004, 48), this system has assumed a hegemonic status. But no system of power is absolute. In this vein, Lind and Barham caution us not to overlook the symbolic exchanges. Otherwise, "something important to humanity is lost if market rhetoric becomes (or is considered to be) the sole rhetoric of human affairs" (2004, 51; cf. Radin 1996, 122). Lind and Barham are concerned with the implications of "a world-view that would consider all elements of social life to be subject to objectification, fungibility, commensurability, and ultimately a dollar value price" (51).

Local people's efforts to go beyond the materiality of food were brought home to me during a brief visit to a rural area (Bamyan). I had accompanied some colleagues from an international aid agency. Just as we were about to depart, a family that we had visited insisted that we stay for lunch. Firoz, the host, called his wife, who was working in the

potato field, and asked her to serve lunch. Within ten minutes, she prepared a yogurt-based dish served with homemade naan. She graciously
shared the recipe with me. When I inquired as to why they went through
the trouble of serving lunch when they themselves were not well-to-do,
my Afghan colleague responded, "Whether they have dry bread or an
expensive meat dish, they will share. This is how food is eaten in this
country." This is an inviolable characteristic that makes us human (*in-
shan*) not discounting the fact that food is not shared indiscriminately.
Reciprocity is certainly taken into account; a meal invitation is extended
on the grounds that it will be reciprocated. Social ties are not detached
from instrumental value as one comes to know what resources to tap into
that will be beneficial. Oftentimes, I heard of neighbours and relatives
not invited to functions because of strained relationships.

Social gatherings are held on a regular basis, however reduced they
may be in scale. Rites of passage and festivals are celebrated in small ways
depending on the circumstances of the families. Wedding parties are the
highlight, observed through the tradition of mutual sharing and borrow-
ing on trust. However, the important point to note is that people's ability
to foster social relationships has been undermined by prolonged war.
The women often made the comment: "We no longer get together the
way we used to." Consider the example of Eid celebrations.

The Festivals of Eid

Muslims celebrate two Eid festivals annually: Eid ul-Fitr and Eid ul-Adha.
Eid ul-Fitr falls in the month of Ramadan, designated as the month of
fasting observed from dawn to dusk. Before the sun rises, families eat
breakfast (a spread consisting of fruit, cheese, butter, eggs, and juice).
While the women attend to their regular household chores (e.g., tend-
ing to the young children, taking care of the garden, weaving, sewing,
maintaining kinship ties), they pay special attention to two activities: preparing food for Iftar (the breaking of the fast) along with the main meal,
and the recitation of the Qur'an jointly with their kin network. Close
relatives and friends may be invited for Iftar, which is reciprocated. The
end of Ramadan is marked by the celebration of Eid. On this day, a special spread is prepared by the women consisting of dried and fresh fruits,
a variety of nuts, and cakes and cookies. Families and neighbours visit
each other to exchange greetings and partake in the food laid out on the
desterkhan. Visiting is governed by norms. The elderly, the sick, and families who have lost a loved one are given priority. Tensions and conflict

between families are resolved through visits and the sharing of food laid out on the *desterkhan*. Prophet Ebrahim's intended sacrifice of his son marks the celebration of the Eid ul-Adha. On this occasion, a lamb or a goat is slaughtered, and the meat is divided into three portions. The first portion is for the immediate family, and the second one for the network of kith and kin. The third one is distributed to the poor.

The above profile of the Eid festivals is drawn from observations made by the elderly women in the households that I visited. The profile refers to life before the war. Though it is general, it is of value as it throws light on, in the words of Salima, "How our celebrations have changed because of the wars in our country." She explained that now (as opposed to before) the celebrations are small: "We do not invite many people as everything is expensive." She noted that even the meat that is distributed is very little, and families have to add lots of potatoes and vegetables to stretch it. I often noticed women's resourcefulness in substituting green lentils and vegetables for meat. Zarin observed that Eid has become like an "ordinary day," stating, "If we want to go out as a family, we need Afs30 for transport and Afs50 for ice cream. We do not have the money." Many of the women are presently engaged in income-generating activities from home, such as crafts work, weaving, sewing, and preparing food for commercial purposes. This work leaves them with little time to participate in the Qur'anic readings, compromising their spiritual and social relationships. Following the readings, women exchange notes on multiple subjects such as childrearing, health, weddings, and food, among others. Below I share my observations on my visits on the occasion of Eid ul-Fitr.

Rehmat invited me to visit a couple of families to say Eid Mubarak (greetings) to her kith and kin. The first family had a generous spread on the *desterkhan*: pomegranates, apples (yellow, green, and red), a variety of melons, grapes, and pears. Dried fruit, pistachios, cashew nuts, almonds, raisins, and walnuts were decoratively placed on two plates. Three kinds of store-bought cakes and biscuits were arranged in between the plates of fruit. Over a cup of tea, we learned that our host, Faizal, was a returnee. Four married brothers and their families live together; the brothers own a clothing store. Though well-to-do, Faizal was acutely aware of the devastation that his country had been subject to. He remembered the effect on his family:

> My two sisters were married young. They were only fourteen and fifteen years old. This is because we were scared that the Taliban would come and get them. I had an older brother. He left school to earn [money] as my

father did not earn enough. They are not in this world anymore. The people of Afghanistan have seen too much pain and sorrow. We all remember
the noises (*sada*) of bombs and rockets. I will never forget the tears of my
sisters when they got married. We have very bad memories of the wars and
we will never forget them. Many people had to go hungry for so many days.
There was no work, and it was not safe to go out.

Note how Faizal inscribes his story into a testimonial social landscape
rendering it more powerful. As Gulsoon stated, "It did not happen
to me. It happened to everybody."

The situation was very different in the other families I visited. They too
had a *desterkhan* laden with special foods, but it was greatly reduced. The
fruit comprised apples and bananas. Instead of nuts, there were chick-
peas, raisins, sunflower seeds, and a homemade cake – less expensive
items. The quality and variety of the fruit and nuts presented depended
on the economic situation of the family. The families highlighted the
narrative of the loss of lives, displacement, and erosion of livelihood.

Both the abundant and the impoverished *desterkhan* evoked memories: the former of what life was like and the latter of what life has become. I am cognizant of not imposing a polarized scenario. The women
themselves divided their lives into before (pre-war) and after without
being romantic. Farida summarized the sentiment of other women: "Life
was hard but not harsh. And the hard life was accompanied by good
times. But now the harsh life does not seem to end. The curtain is not
falling on it. Our celebrations are like normal days." Rashida recalled
how on the occasion of Eid, they used to wear new clothes and jewellery
and have abundant food: "When we were children, we got Eidi money,
and we would buy sweets and ice cream. I cannot do the same for my
children." These observations fall under the rubric of "wounding events"
to use Kadar's (2005) words. When festivals are rendered into ordinary
days, and when they "cannot go to weddings because we do not have nice
clothes," the women's recollections suggest the extent to which their social and cultural lives have been compromised. Not being able to engage in active relationships with others and, therefore, be part of a social
world must be considered as extreme – violence of the self, as Hastrup
(2003) expresses it.

What I have presented above includes the resourcefulness of feminin-
ity, to use Duruz's (2005) words. But the women are engaged in another
task, and this is memory work. The women do not merely remember the
past – they recall it to highlight a lack in the present. The lack concerns,

memories of the war

for example, the unavailability of meat that encapsulates the larger world of social relationships. As the women informed me repeatedly, without meat (*gosht*) they cannot celebrate special occasions; without meat they cannot entertain guests; without meat they cannot have a familial/communal feast. In short, their family life is compromised in the absence of what has been a staple diet for generations. Whether it is lamb, mutton, beef, or chicken, meat is of symbolic value. Not being able to afford meat undermines their ability to be part of an extended social world critical to their well-being. Yet, the women's everyday work of cooking keeps the fire of the hearth burning. In the words of Naseem: "And it is this fire that will be recalled by families when Afghanistan has better days. This is how we survived, and this we hope will be a story that our children will remember." Fatima expressed the sentiment: "So far as I can light the stove, I can serve something to my family even if it is just soft rice and lentils." It is important to note that the women are not able to spend much time at the hearth – the hub of their lives as they had known it. They spend less time cooking as they prepare fewer dishes with sparser ingredients. Nevertheless, they keep the fire burning however diminished it may be, and through it they keep alive the cultural import of food evident in their concern to maintain social relationships however reduced they may be.

① NO LOSS OF HOPE
② CONTINUING/ PUSHING THROUGH WAR.

Vendors with Handcarts

In the course of our conversations, some of the women made reference to the vendors with carts or food vendors (*karachiwan*) from whom they would obtain vegetables. A closer look revealed their presence on the streets of Kabul. You cannot miss them. The carts are used to transport goods, to carry cement and stones for construction sites, or to sell produce and other items such as clothes and shoes. The carts are a reminder that "this country does not have peace. Our lives have been destroyed" (Sherbaz). His observations capture a situation that has come about because "so many people's lives have been turned upside down by the wars in Afghanistan," added Amin. Salima noted that there were "not so many carts on the streets before," meaning in the pre-war period. The carts are an icon of the "destruction of Afghanistan," a term used repeatedly by the women. The often-repeated phrase, "The cart must keep moving" refers to the vendors' need to be mobile to earn a meagre living. Yet, the vendors have a base in the neighbourhoods where they live and are known. According to the women, it is not uncommon for families

to purchase vegetables from their vendors in their respective neighbourhoods. Other than being cheaper, especially at the end of the day, and
more convenient, the vendor sells on credit when necessary. Salima put
it this way: "We always pay back later. It is nice to know that in times of
need, we can get some produce." Other women explained that they get
the produce on credit when they have guests. The vendors, in turn, bor-
row money from close-knit neighbours in times of crisis or to pay for
wedding or funeral expenses.

In their respective neighbourhoods, the vendors are not only shop-
keepers in the informal economy, but persons with familial and work
histories. And these histories entail a network of relationships with, in
the words of one vendor, "persons who were known to our grandparents
and with persons who are now their children." Relationships, as a matter
of course, are embedded in memories. Who lived here, what happened
to such a person, what were the good and bad times that were shared,
and so on; the most vivid memories were that of war. Here are two stories
that Nazleen and Khulsum shared with me, respectively.

Nazleen was squatted on the floor cutting green peppers and onions.
There was a large amount. When I asked her what she was going to do
with the produce, she said, "I will make pickles. I will give some to my
sisters and keep the rest for my family." In the course of the conversation,
she informed me that the vendor (Ebrahim) who sold her the produce
has a tragic story. His three brothers died when the Taliban attacked
their home in Pul i Khumri. They had a farm. Nazleen recalled:

> The mother and all the brothers were working on the farm. She saw the
> Taliban coming. She shouted and told her sons to hide. Ebrahim was close
> to the house. He hid under the bed. It was too late for the other brothers.
> They were shot in the head. The mother refuses to leave the farm. She says
> she has to guard the bodies of her three children who are buried there. She
> prays over the graves.

Once a month, Ebrahim visits the farm to pick up seasonal vegetables.
This time he had brought green peppers and onions from the farm
which has been reduced in size as it was not spared destruction. The
mother keeps alive the memory of her children by remaining on the site
where they were killed; the brother keeps alive the memory of violence
through the produce that he sells.

Whenever I visited Khulsum, I would say "Salaam" (greeting of peace)
to a vendor (Jaffer) selling only bananas from his cart. Jaffer is visually

impaired. People who buy bananas from him leave Afs2 per banana in a box placed in a corner. Khulsum informed me that except for his daughter, he lost his family members in the wars and also due to sickness. His daughter helps to set up the cart. Images of loss and recovery (survival in a social milieu of trust) are captured in this story. Having heard Jaffer's story, I chatted with him a couple of times. He informed me that he lost his father in the civil war, hit by a bullet on his way to work. His mother fell sick and passed away soon after. The family could not get medical help for her. "It was war. What kind of help can you get?" he said. His two brothers were killed by the Taliban. "Gunshot wounds," he recalled. "They were in the house. The Taliban demanded money that we did not have. So they just killed them, like that." War and violence do not spare civilians. The image of Jaffer selling bananas from the cart is a _reminder_ of what the people of Afghanistan have endured and continue to endure – surviving on the bare minimum. (memories)

Each vendor had a story that was not substantially different from their neighbour's. The common theme was loss of lives and possessions. It was this shared experience that blurred the boundary between sellers and buyers at particular moments. I accompanied Khadija's twelve-year-old son Rahim when he went to pick up vegetables. The vendor's cart was five minutes from her house. Following greetings, as no transaction takes place without a reciprocal exchange of good wishes, this exchange took place:

VENDOR (SHERBAZ): What would you like to buy today?
RAHIM: My mother wants peas, onions, spinach, and potatoes.
SHERBAZ: Shall I put these in one bag? It comes to Afs35.
RAHIM: I have Afs20. I will bring the rest of the money in the evening. I am
   going to work [selling plastic bags] in the afternoon.
RAHIM: Where is your friend, Ahmed?
SHERBAZ: He has not come today. He is not well.

This conversation is of interest as it reveals a model where economic transaction is not absolute and all-encompassing. The cultural exchange softens the market metaphor of buy and sell.

Some of the vendors sell fruit (_mewa_) as well. But it is rarely purchased, as the women I talked to found fruit to be too expensive. Neatly arranged in the cart, the fruit embodies past memories. "We used to have fruit every day. Now we only have vegetables. I give naan to my children for a snack. They should be having an apple or some kind of fruit," noted

↗ HoPe .

Bilkis. The contrast between "used to" and "now" is sharp. "They should be having ..." refers to a hoped-for future.

Vegetable Patch (Shadow of the Kitchen Garden)

In many of the homes that I visited, I noticed vegetable patches (*kurd sabzi*) in the yard. Some of them were tiny and barely noticeable. Yet, it is on these patches that the women grow two to three vegetables such as green onions, green peppers, tomatoes, peas, and carrots. Some of the women, if space permits, keep a goat or two for milk. The vegetable patch along with the animals serves a twofold purpose. The first one is evident. The produce helps women to stretch their budgets and also maintain the traditional practice of exchange. For example, onions and peppers could be exchanged for eggs. The second purpose is to keep alive the memory of home life as they have known it. When I asked Siteza how she takes care of two goats in the yard, she said:

> I grew up with goats. I have looked after mother-goats who were expecting. We had a good-sized farm. We had many animals. I used to milk goats and even cows with my mother. We would get up early, say our *namaz* (prayers) and then get fresh milk. My mother taught me how to make yogurt and cheese. I still do this. This is my way of remembering a life we have lost. I am trying to create a home in a place that has holes from bullets. We have to live according to how Allah keeps us. My mother taught me to have faith. I am thankful that I have the goats. It gives me the feeling of being at home even when half of the house has been destroyed.

Siteza is not the only one who engages in memory work from the tiny space of her yard shared with other women. Jamila remembered a small garden where her family grew one crop – potatoes or onions – on a rotating basis. She acquired the skill of maximizing the soil that she considered to be hard. She related:

> It was not easy to grow on the soil in our garden. I learned from my father when to plant, what kind of fertilizer to use, and when to harvest. I am now able to grow potatoes in this patch. It reminds me of our garden and my family life. I give potatoes to my neighbour. She gives me apples or peas.

Rahima did not grow up on a farm. Her patch where she grows lettuce and peas makes her remember her uncle's farm in a rural area. She used to visit him: "He told me: 'If you want to remember Afghanistan, you have to remember what we grow here. Our country is built on its soil [meaning agriculture].'" For Rahima, the patch is a way to remember the past in the present; the past is the story of Afghanistan and its connection to land.

The three ethnographic sites (the hearth, the vendors with their carts, and the vegetable patch) discussed in this chapter capture the scars of war. The hearth is the place where minimal food is prepared filled with memories of the pre-war life. The sharp contrast between the before (pre-war) and the after (ongoing conflict) is not portrayed in nostalgic terms. Rather, it constitutes a political critique of the violence of war in the inner recesses of life. It also helps to bring to light feminine resourcefulness (the work of recovery) illustrated in the metaphor, "the hearth fire will not be extinguished."

The vendors' handcarts also illustrate the enactment of violence in the inner recesses of life. The vendors' mass presence on the streets of Kabul remains unnoticed politically; no measures have been taken to remedy their situation of living from hand to mouth. But their close-knit ties in their respective neighbourhoods reveal a model of transaction that goes beyond the market metaphor of buy and sell. In the form of molecular change, this model makes it possible for families to survive and foster social relationships. The vendors, like their neighbours, embody memories of violence in war.

As a shadow of the former kitchen garden, the vegetable patch represents the lived memory of violence. Unnoticed, it serves a twofold purpose. First, it stands for feminine resourcefulness based on gender and a generational stock of knowledge. Second, barely noticed and yielding limited produce, the patch captures violence in the inner recesses of life. It is a signature of devastation.

In this chapter, I have argued that food infused with memory work has the potential to make violence knowable in the inner recesses of life. As activities performed on a daily basis, food and memory work also reveal the process of recovery that could form the basis for remedial work from the bottom up. Engaged anthropology requires that we do not allow violence in the inner recesses of life to escape our attention. Unacknowledged forms of violence and bottom-up attempts at recovery can remain buried. I continue to explore this theme in relation to foodscapes at Valley View, the site of my field research in Burnaby, Canada. Foodscapes refer to the active and ongoing interconnection between food, places, and people. There are three reasons for adopting this term: as an everyday activity connected to the larger world, foodscapes allow us to observe discontinuities and disruptions caused by protracted conflicts. Second, foodscapes is a key site for exploring local worlds as these unfold through "biographies of food" – a term used by Smith and Jehlicka (2007). Third, foodscapes (as opposed to food) captures a larger terrain signalling its trajectory across time and space.

5
Foodscapes

In chapter 4, I explored three ethnographic sites (the hearth, the vendor's cart, and the vegetable patch) to illustrate the relationship between memory work and food. These mediums, I argued, reveal the workings of violence in the inner recesses of life as well as survival strategies within spaces of devastation. In this chapter, I continue to explore this theme to highlight an additional point: the intricate ways in which Afghanistan (*there*) and Canada (*here*) are interconnected. By way of illustration, I focus on three sites from my ethnographic research in Valley View (Burnaby): the street, the home, and the food bank.

A Walk down the Street of Valley View

The area of Valley View encapsulates the multicultural face of Canada. A walk down the main street reveals men and women shopping, going to work, walking their children to school, or heading to a program at one of the local community organizations. As you come to know their countries of origin, you discover that the majority are refugees (used interchangeably here with "newcomers") from war-torn countries such as Zaire, Sudan, Iraq, Afghanistan, Uganda, and Eritrea. Many of the newcomers reside in the low-income housing complex behind the street. Hidden by trees and side streets, the low-rise complex of one- or two-bedroom apartments is barely visible. And it is only when you cross over to the residential area that you notice that the complex is rundown and in need of repairs and paint. The balconies are filled with household things, such as bicycles, boxes, and old mattresses.

The street of Valley View embodies multiple scripts. The first is that of multiculturalism. The nation state of Canada takes pride in having accommodated peoples from different countries. But the federal policy of multiculturalism was instituted in 1971, not so much to recognize the presence of ethnic minorities from other countries, but to contain the tensions between the two charter groups: the English and the French. This overriding framework gave little space to minorities; hence, the policy proved to be problematic right from the outset creating a division between the private and the public sectors. As Li (2003) has expressed it, ethnic minorities are "expected to conform to Canada's official languages in public institutions, but are encouraged to pursue an ethnic culture and lifestyle of their choice in their private life ... Thus despite the multicultural policy, the norms and practices of the two charter groups prevail in the public sphere, and the policy does not provide a viable option for cultural minorities nor new immigrants to escape the forces of conformity in major institutions" (134). This half-hearted policy has far-reaching consequences as it perpetuates racism on the grounds that minorities do not enjoy substantive citizenship rights except what is accorded them in a legal document. As Thobani (2011) has stated, "The definition of what it means to be a rightful and legitimate Canadian is and has always been a question of race" (vii).

The above observations illuminate the second script embedded in contradictions.[1] The main street of Valley View contains two types of stores: low-end and high-end. The relatively few low-end stores include small produce stores run by Afghans, a hairdresser, a dollar store, a cafe, a secondhand furniture store, and a clothing thrift store. The high-end shops include two large groceries, a couple of hairdressers, a posh cafe, restaurants, a gym, a wholesale produce store, and service-oriented businesses. There is no sharp demarcation between the two types of stores in the area. Blurring of boundaries occurs as people shop around the city, not only for bargains but also for social value. Rashida, for example, stated that most of the time she buys clothing from the thrift store. However, on the festive occasion of Eid, she said, "I go to the department stores in Metro-town to buy new clothes for my children. Otherwise it is not like Eid."

Given the high value of real estate in Greater Vancouver, high-end businesses tend to set up shop in this relatively less expensive area. And they are able to attract shoppers, as Valley View is accessible via a couple of highways (not named here to maintain the anonymity of the place). In short, the underprivileged families from the nearby areas shop from the limited number of low-end shops. The high-end shops are economically not accessible to them although they live in the vicinity. The newcomers have limited income. Government-sponsored refugees receive $900 plus per month, depending on the size of the family, for one year only. Each family has many expenses to cover. First, they have to pay back the government loan for their travel to Canada. Second, rent takes up three-quarters of their monies. The rest is for food and household expenses. The third script concerns the multiple ways in which the newcomers remake their worlds. Low-end stores receive some foods which have already passed their shelf life, particularly fruit, vegetables, and frozen foods. The unstated premise is that, in the words of one research participant, "people who are poor will purchase these dated items." And, indeed, they are purchased. As the director of a service program put it, "The working poor and those who are on social assistance cannot afford to shop elsewhere." It is through the purchase of these foods with a short shelf life that some of the women manage to feed their families in Canada. I came to know two family-owned Afghan stores well through my regular weekly visits over a period of two years (2010–12). I shopped at these stores for nuts and dried fruit, during which time I talked to the owners (Ali and his wife Rehmet, and Hassan and his wife Zahra) as well to the customers, who are largely from the war-torn countries mentioned above.

The two stores are unique in the Valley View streetscape. They carry produce (vegetables and fruit), dry products (such as tea, beans, rice, and lentils), and dairy products (cheese, milk, and eggs). They also sell Afghan and Middle Eastern foods, such as dried fruit (figs, apricots, and dates), a variety of artisan breads, and sweets and spices. Additional items for sale include Pakistani and South Asian spices and lentils. International telephone cards are widely sold, illustrating the connection between *here* (*inja*) and *there* (*anja*). The uniqueness of the stores is not exclusively a function of the products for sale; it is also attributed to the social interactions embedded within the commercial transactions. These interactions do not take a lot of time. They are quick, but they contain depth and meaning. They echo a form of practice rather than an exclusive physical space, not unknown in the marketplaces in other societies, including Afghanistan. Here, markets and social relationships are mutually constitutive (Elyachar 2005). Consider the following examples.

"Burning of the Copies of the Qur'an"

My first example comes from the incident on 22 February 2012, when US soldiers at Bagram airbase burned copies of the Qur'an, leading to protests and riots within and outside Afghanistan. An Afghan man, who had come to the store in Valley View to buy naan, asked Ali if his family was safe. Ali responded with the comment, "There is trouble everywhere. My family is asking when will there be peace in the country." When I asked Ali what he thought of the incident, he said, "*The whole of Afghanistan is burning*" (original emphasis). He continued, "Both my family and myself are mentally fatigued. The war has gone on for too long." He noted that whenever there is a bomb blast in Afghanistan, he picks up his phone and calls his family to ask them if they are all right: "Only then I don't worry." News from Afghanistan and other parts of the Middle East provide the forum for the customers and storeowners to tell their own stories and articulate their concerns over the well-being of their families over there. Incidents over *there* are felt over *here* like earthquake tremors. Through a powerful metaphor, Ali draws the attention of the audience (over here), equating the burning of the Qur'an with that of the whole of Afghanistan. At the same time, he makes a plea for peace, once again evoking the attention of the people over here. Ali's comment echoes the sentiments of an Afghan anthropologist, Anila Daulatzai (2006, 2008), who notes that it is time that we acknowledge the long-time suffering of the people of Afghanistan. In Ali's store, such acknowledgment happens casually, during conversation, but it carries impact. I heard Ali reiterate the two points on suffering (*ranj*) and peace (*solh*) to other customers on several occasions, phrased differently according to particular contexts. Allow me to introduce a second example.

A Scarred Body

I was in the process of paying for Afghan figs in Hassan's store when a customer walked in. He asked me if I was from Uganda. "Yes, but how did you guess?" I inquired. He said, "It is your accent." In response to my question on how he had fared under Idi Amin, responsible for the expulsion of South Asians and the killing and torture of hundreds of Africans, he lifted the sleeve of his right arm and showed us several scars. This action, in turn, triggered memories for Hassan, as both he and his uncle had been tortured by the Taliban. Hassan stated:

> I have scars on my back. The Taliban took me when I was [out] walking and put me in jail. They released me once they realized that they had the wrong man. They did the same to my uncle. After this, we left Afghanistan. I realized how badly the country was destroyed in every way.

Within the limited space of the store and in the context of a food purchase, personal stories of violence involving two countries had taken place. The sharing of such stories becomes part of the repertoire of memories that the newcomers relate. These memories are not frozen in time; they are context-specific. Memories of violence in war lead to greater awareness that something is amiss with the world, revealing several points. First, memories are testimonial in nature; their personalized remembering renders them powerful. Second, the scars evoke the question of healing. Are there strategies and practices in place that would make it possible for people to reconstitute their worlds following devastation? I posit that these questions are not answered in a totalizing way. The responses emerge gradually in contexts of everyday life through means that bind us together as human beings such as the foodscapes that capture the larger world of power and politics. This brings me to my third example, on naan (Afghan bread).

I have to buy all this bread to feed my family. It was the same in Afghanistan.

– Roya

Bread[2] (naan) is a staple and supplementary item in Afghan diets. Served at breakfast, lunch, and dinner, it is eaten with a main dish. Cooked in a *tandoor* (clay oven) and eaten fresh, its scent emanates from bakeries and also homes. Large and oval or rectangular in shape, it is relatively inexpensive. Three to ten loaves are bought at a time. With prolonged war, bread has undergone a shift from being a supplementary food to a main food source owing to its affordability, though it, too, has gone up in price from Afs3.00 to Afs6.00 per loaf. In Afghanistan, some of the families only had bread and tea for breakfast and in dire circumstances for dinner as well. I also observed mothers giving bread to their children for a snack rather than fruit. This is the context for Roya's comment cited at the beginning of this section. It contains a political critique in that, when it comes to feeding one's family, there is no substantive difference between *here* and *there*. They ate a lot of bread there, and they eat a lot of bread here because of their limited economic capacity. Over there, Roya's husband had casual work; over here, he has been laid off. Her two children are working part-time while attending high school to help with the family finances.

Roya's narrative is not atypical. The situation that Afghans face in Canada has been well-summarized by Khan (2001). Citing the case of Naima, a refugee in Canada, Khan notes, "Her life is spent in struggling with under-employment and unemployment, lack of affordable housing, and lack of settlement programs to help her heal from the trauma of war and fragmentation of her country" (15). Khan further argues that it is necessary to identify "first-world complicity which Razack argues we must talk about 'if the lives of refugees are to make any sense to us'" (1998, 48, quoted in Khan 2001, 15). Talking about one's needs and one's situation in contexts where a concerned listener is present is certainly how Valley View community members thrive in the face of adversities. This brings me to my fourth example of critical information exchange in the midst of commercial transactions.

Critical Information Exchange

Following my exchange of greetings, *salaam alikumm*, with Ali, I went to one of the shelves to get some walnuts. A customer walked in and asked Ali if he knew of any job vacancies. Ali pulled out a card from his shirt pocket, and said, "Here take this. This person left me his card only yesterday. He is looking for someone to work with him." I asked Ali if he typically helps his customers in this way. He replied, "All the time, when-ever they ask me." Ali is multilingual, and knows Dari, Pashtun, English, French, and Urdu. He verbally translates letters for Afghan customers from English to Dari or Pashtun. He also assists customers in writing resumes. In the course of our conversation, he said, "It is only because of this service work that I enjoy running this store. Otherwise, it is not interesting for me."

The services offered by Ali are not one-sided. Two critical issues came up in conversations and are discussed in fragments, during the course of purchases being made. The first issue concerns the reluctance of Immigration Canada to issue visitor visas to family members wishing to travel from Afghanistan. Ali explained, "I have not seen my parents for six years. They [Immigration Canada] will not allow them to come here for a visit. They think that they will stay here because of violence in Afghanistan." In the course of conversations with customers, Ali has learned that he is not alone. Canadian Afghan families have been unable to bring over their family members for a visit, especially parents. A few suggestions have been put forward: they could pay a deposit with their application; they could include their residency or citizenship certificate as a guarantee; they could get a professional person to act as a guaran-tor. Exploring different solutions to an impending issue is the first step towards effecting potential change, both immediate and long term.[3]

The second issue is that of the hijab (head scarf), an icon of Muslim women's oppression in the West. On the ground reality is much more complex.[4] My observations are based on interactions at Hassan's shop while Zahra was on duty. Zahra used to wear the hijab when she first came to Canada, seven years ago. Noticing that people were staring at her and that she could not find work, she removed it. She related, "They would call me for an interview and when they saw my hijab, they would not call me back. At first, I did not make the connection, [but] after some time, I removed it." Her own experiences made her pay close attention to the stories of her female customers. One woman stated that she would never remove the hijab even if this meant that she did not get a job. A second woman was torn, and said, "If I wear the hijab, people do not hire me. If I do not wear the hijab, my Afghan friends give me looks as to how I can give up my identity." A third woman related that wearing the hijab earns her respect from her work colleagues: "They treat me nice. I don't know if they think that I am oppressed." These conversations emerged gradually over time, and in bits and pieces. As I pieced together the whole picture, I could see that to a large extent, the hijab embodied memories. The women remembered how the wearing of the hijab became an issue under the Taliban regime (1996–2001) when the burqa (garment that covers the body from head to feet) was imposed through injunction. Hejira, a regular customer stated, "We were surprised that the hijab is an issue in Canada." Note how this one sentence establishes a connection between *here* and *there* – memory work. The women remember their oppression under the Taliban. Some of the women questioned as to how free they actually feel in Canada, given that this country has presented itself as democratic. If we are to complicate the socially constructed divide between *here* and *there*, we need to introduce a historical context succinctly expressed by Khan (2001) with reference to Naima (an Afghan Canadian): "And Naima's tormented tale of violence and exile brought about by the situation in Afghanistan does not end when she leaves her country. It continues in Canada where she faces exclusion, underemployment, and racism" (14).

My ethnographic research at the site of the stores reveals that people from war-torn countries embody memories of violence both *here* and *there*. These memories are rendered politically invisible as they do not make their way into the circuits of power – nationally or globally. The dominant narrative of the saviour script defines Afghan women as needing to be saved from the brutality of their culture and religion, in a country where the superpowers have been active players advancing their own

political and economic agendas. What renders women's memory work –
active and fluid – powerful is that it is triggered by their immediate experiences in Canada. How else can we explain Roya's comment that both in
Canada and in Afghanistan she has had to buy lots of bread to feed her
children? In the context of everyday life, where shopping, cooking, and
the consumption of food is central and visceral, her comment contains a
political edge. My reading suggests that the women (not excluding men)
in their own ways are engaged in making the experiences of violence in
the inner recesses of life knowable. This process does not exclude the
reconstitution of everyday life.

Memory work, storytelling, and food consumption are human experiences. They engage us all. When a woman states that she was forced to
wear the burqa in Afghanistan and that her choice of wearing the hijab
in Canada subjects her to racism/Islamophobia, she links the two countries in a manner that has not been previously imagined. The testimonial
mode, whereby one person's memory captures the situation of the cohort, is powerful. As Felman (1992) expresses it, "A life-testimony is not
simply a testimony to a private life, but a point of conflation between text
and life, a textual testimony which can *penetrate us like an actual life*" (2,
original emphasis). Food evokes the lived reality of *here* and *there*. Before
exploring the second theme on the inner space of the home, I would
like to further explore the question of remembering the lived realities,
and how these evoke the attention of a listening audience.

Remembering Lived Realities

When Najiba (a customer) walked into Ali's store, she looked worried.
Rahemet was at the cashier. When she inquired as to what was bother-
ing Najiba, she said that her husband had lost his job. He was engaged
in construction work with a small Canadian company. She related the
following story briefly in the store, and later to me on the pavement, to
illustrate the point that their difficulties were not coming to an end as
they had hoped:

> I came to Canada for survival. The reason why I left my country was that
> there was war [the civil war]. The civilians were in the middle and the two
> parties were fighting on both sides and we were exposed to so many explo-
> sions and different types of weapons. One time, the war [bombing] contin-
> ued for forty-eight hours. My son was only six months old. And we could not
> leave our home; even inside the house, it was not safe. I spent all the time

in the washroom, and I put my child in the bathtub to protect him. And after forty-eight hours, I realized that I did not have any strength to stand. My knees were shaking, and there was broken glass everywhere. It was really hard. My husband decided that it was time to leave the country. I am not keeping well here because of all the worries.

Najiba's act of remembrance does not take place in a vacuum. It has a context. The women I conversed with stated that they came to Canada with the expectation that there would be opportunities for them to move forward. They also emphasized the importance of jobs without which "life is an everyday struggle, just as it was in Afghanistan" (Najiba). She continued, "If we can have a good life here, we will not remember all the horrible things that happened to us in our country," a point of view reiterated by other women.

Effecting Change through Food

When my children (two daughters and a son) joined the [primary] school, I informed the teacher, "We do not eat pork." They would give the other children pork sandwiches; my children got cucumber and tomato sandwiches, also used for the pork sandwiches. They did not do anything special for my children. My children sensed it. I had to go three times to the school and inform them that my children should not get the feeling of being left out. They now add beef or cheese. (Naseem, in the context of purchasing halal meat from Hassan's store)[5]

The above is a food story revealing the dynamics of the larger forces, and the paradox of advancing the image of Canada as a multicultural society yet not accommodating its culturally diverse population in ways that matter: like the everyday consumption of food. It is through the medium of food that Naseem took on the role of advocate for both her own children and other Muslim children in the school. When I asked her if she thought the beef in the sandwiches was halal, she said, "This is the next topic that will have to wait as the school is just accepting the idea of serving different foods."[6]

Mankekar's work on Indian grocery stores in the diasporic space of San Francisco is of interest. Presenting a layered account, she highlights three main themes. First, "Indian grocery stores invoke and produce powerful discourse of home, family, and community – all of which are contested, and all of which are gendered in important ways" (2002, 92).

Second, the stores constitute sites where "Indian culture" is reconfigured and produced outside the nation state of India, paving the way for
the ethnography of transnationalism with its potential to subvert state
policing of territorial boundaries. Third, the polyvocality of commodities bought and consumed in the stores engenders "a complex set of
emotions (ranging from nostalgia, to ambivalence, to open antagonism)
refracted by the haunting presence of the familiar – its loss, its absent
presence, and, in a few cases, its attempted retrieval." Echoing insights
offered by Mankekar, I continue to focus on two critical moments: remembering the losses in the country of origin and reliving the losses in
the country of settlement of the newcomers.

Inner Space of the Home

As was the case in Kabul, my visits to the homes of the women took place
in the mornings. The women had more free time to talk then, as their
husbands had left for work (or their job search) and except for the tod-
dlers, their children were at school. This does not exclude widows with
children. We sat on sofas with throw covers, the purpose of which is typically to increase their life span. The reverse was the case in the homes I
visited; the throw covers hide the secondhand sofas and their worn-out
sections. The carpets were also covered, with red Afghan rugs (*qalen*)
serving a twofold purpose.[7] First, brought from Afghanistan or a second
country (Pakistan or Iran), the red rugs provide a homelike atmosphere.
Second, the rugs cover the worn-out carpets in the rundown apartments.
The sofas and the carpets represent the lack and scarcity that the women
and their families experienced in Afghanistan. In their country of settlement in Canada, the women in my study are also subject to deprivation.
The women that I visited not only live in rundown apartments with worn-
out sofas and worn-out carpets, which they have creatively covered, but
they are cramped. The research participants and their families of four to
six children, on average, live in two-bedroom apartments equipped with
small kitchens, reminiscent of the tiny space of the hearth from which
they prepared meals in Afghanistan. The women have a limited budget
derived from government assistance and/or the low-paid work of family
members.

The above profile formed the backdrop of my observations and conversations with the women. As was the case in Afghanistan, my initial research in the homes focused on meal patterns. While these yield insights

on memory work revealing processes of adaptation, including generational negotiations, the subject matter of meal patterns was not of interest to the women I interacted with. They responded politely to some
questions, but over time, I observed that their interest lay in recounting
critical incidents that captured crisis situations, where food was often the
unsaid script. I present both sets of data below. First, I include a typical
profile of the everyday meals, followed by three critical incidents.

Everyday Meals[8]

I wake up at five o'clock in the morning. I say my *namaz*, and then I go into
the kitchen [to] prepare breakfast. When we first came to Canada, we had a
good breakfast just as in Afghanistan when there was peace. We had cheese,
eggs, bread (naan), yogurt, and fruit. Now with our limited budget, my husband and I have toast and chai. The children have cereal and milk. They
are also in a hurry, [so] there is not much time for breakfast. On weekends,
we have eggs. I also make lunch for my husband. Most of the time, he takes
cheese sandwiches; if there is leftover food, I pack it for him. Two of my children who are in primary school get their lunch in school. My older children
[two] attend high school. I make them sandwiches. They never take Afghan
food. They ask for meat. I tell them, "I will include meat some other time." I
do not want to tell them that we cannot afford this too often. Once or twice
a month we have meat.

Nashrin's account is of interest as, other than capturing the meal patterns in the households of her cohort (not overlooking variations), it
reveals three main themes. First, and poignantly, it establishes a connection between *here* and *there*. In the initial/honeymoon period in their
new country, the family remembered the peaceful time in Afghanistan through the medium of food. This time is contrasted with life in
war-ravaged Afghanistan and the settlement struggles they experience
in Canada. Fundamentally, in both countries, the women's (and their
families') experiences have been informed by limited food budgets.
Nashrin's comment on the affordability of meat reflects the same situation prevalent among women in my study in Afghanistan. The second
theme revealed is the discomfort of the older children to consume Afghan food in the public space of the school. This shows the lack of ac-
ceptance of the food of the Other, except in situations of cosmopolitan
gastronomy where it is accepted at a distance – that is, in the safe space

of an "ethnic" restaurant. Shireen put it this way, "No, no, our children would never take Afghan food for lunch. They would be laughed at by other children. They would say, 'What kind of food are you eating?' or something like that." Echoing Naseem's account in the store, Dolat relayed how she had to make a case that her child is not a vegetarian: "Only then they would include beef in his sandwich instead of pork or just vegetables."[9] Dolat's initiative can be appreciated in the light of the fact that "experience is not the end point but the beginning of an exploration of the relationship between the personal and the social and therefore the political" (Agnew 2007, 6).

The feminist dictum that the personal is political is well captured by food: who prepares it? Where it is consumed and the norms and ideologies that underpin its production and consumption relay the larger story of "which kinds of memories does food have the particular capacity to inscribe, and are there other ways that food may be implicated in a conscious or unconscious forgetting?" (Holtzman 2006, 363).

The third theme in Nashrin's account concerns time schedules dictated by the capitalistic market economy. Ray (2004) shows how the pressure of time to accommodate work schedules, including commute time, has changed the meal cycles and consumption of food among middle-class Bengali Americans in a suburb of Chicago. Breakfast and lunch, he notes, belong to the public sphere while dinner is the preserve of the private world of the Bengalis. A similar pattern prevailed among the Afghan households I visited, with some variations. As was the case in Afghanistan, feminine resourcefulness is at work in these households informed by a limited budget. The women related that three-quarters of their income of $1,200 to $1,400 goes to rent. The dinners that they prepare here have the same baseline of minimal ingredients as in their home country: lentils, rice, less-expensive mainstream bread, and vegetables. They stretch their budget by shopping at different places, including buying the produce from the two Afghan stores. And they also include Canadian foods in their diets to accommodate the needs of their children. Pizza, burgers, and pasta were three popular foods. Adila stated:

It adds variety to our diet. My husband [Amin] wants Afghan foods. Sometimes, I make an Afghan sauce and add it to the pizza and pasta. Other times, I have to prepare two meals: Afghan for Amin and I, and Canadian food for the children. It takes time [but] these foods are not too expensive to make.

Occasionally, the women and their families visit fast food restaurants. In a consumer society, these are not inaccessible. However, there exist additional issues. Maryam explained:

> My children collect coupons and there are special deals. I like to take the children out as they do not have a father. My husband died in the war. One day we went to a pizza place and ordered meat-pizza. When I took a bite, it did not taste right. I asked the waiter if it was pork as I had told him that we do not eat pork. He told me, "No pork." I took a second bite, and again, it did not taste right. I asked a second waiter. He told me, "Yes it was pork (*gosht khok*)." We went home without eating.

How is one to read this incident? Was this negligence on the part of the waiter? Or, can we attribute this incident to the workings of racism and Islamophobia post-9/11? Scholars like Agnew (2007), Razack et al. (2010), and Kim et al. (2012) have put forth the framework of everyday racism, which is systemic and institutionalized. For example, Maryam wears the hijab (head scarf), the visible marker of identity. This aspect could have given rise to the waiter's dismissal of her concern about pork. Visible markers of difference can greatly affect how one is treated. Dolat related that prospective employers did not hire her until she stopped wearing the hijab: "They said 'we will call you back' and they never did. I did not have any choice but to work as a cleaner in Iranian homes. They accepted me wearing the hijab. But they pay me very little money: $8.00 an hour."

Insensitivity to the culinary needs of the Afghans and the exclusion of the hijab from the public sphere, with some exceptions, constitutes a violation of one's humanity. These exclusions undermine the rights of the Afghan women and their families to be part of a wider society. It is in this context of structural vulnerability that Kim et al. (2012) observe, "The ongoing symbolic and material violence levied on supposedly terrifying diasporic bodies are part of the 'War on Terror' and testifies in a very real way to the impossibility of dislodging the process of racial wounding from discourses of Canadian citizenship" (178). In Afghanistan, women's ability to be part of the social world was compromised because of the scarcity of food, especially meat. In Canada, their ability to be part of the social world is compromised because of the lack of acceptability. These experiences of diminished personhood constitute violence in the inner recesses of life. It is not tangible, it is not measured, and it remains unaddressed. For further illustration, I would like to draw upon two critical

incidents, as these take us to the margins of society where food exists in
the form of a silent script.

There were tanks on the streets and helicopters in the sky.

– Malikka

Recounting her childhood, Malikka relayed her father's observations with
reference to the Soviet invasion of Afghanistan. As an anti-communist,
her father felt that it was not safe for the family to stay in one place.
Malikka observed that she never got to know her birthplace of Shirdagh,
and she has only fleeting memories of her childhood in Herat, where the
family lived for two years. During the civil war, from 1992 to 1996, her
family moved to Pakistan and then to Iran. They returned to Afghanistan
during repatriation following the fall of the Taliban in 2001. Life in exile
was difficult. In Iran and in Pakistan, all the family members – Malikka,
her parents, and her four siblings – worked to make ends meet. They
lived from hand to mouth eating simple meals of rice, lentils, beans, and
vegetables. In describing their life, Malikka said, "Because we were illegal
immigrants, I could not attend school. We could not stay in one city as
we would be caught. We lived in Tehran, Mashhad, and Qom." Malikka's
father got her married at a young age to his brother's son, Zulfikar: "I
was not happy, but there was no choice as life was difficult for all of us."
Girls are married off for the reason that there will be one less mouth to
feed, explained Zahra, an elderly woman that I spoke to.

The couple was graced with a daughter. Zulfikar was restless as he did
not want to live in Iran owing to the lack of job opportunities; he went
back to Afghanistan. Advised by a friend, Malikka travelled to Turkey
with her daughter (*dukhtar*): "This was one way through which we could
go to Canada. My daughter was turning six. I had to do something for
her education (*talim*), otherwise she could not attend school, as an illegal immigrant." The Canadian visa application was rejected once, but
went through the second time. She and her daughter arrived in Vancouver in 2004, and with the help of friends she rented an apartment in Valley View. She wanted her husband to join her, and this meant securing
work as per the visa requirement:

Even though I had problems speaking English, I was still able to do most
of the requirements for particular jobs that I applied for. But, when I went
for the interview and they saw that I was wearing the hijab, they told me that
they [would] call me later. None of them did.

Malikka had no choice but to do housework. She took care of an elderly
Iranian woman, and also cleaned Iranian homes. Because of her hijab,
marking her identity as a Muslim woman, she remained confined, even
in terms of work. Malikka stated, "But the pressure of work, school [she
attended ESL classes], and taking care of my daughter affected my mental health (*sehat e rawani*)."

Malikka embodies the scars of the violence of war. First, internal displacement deprived her of her childhood. Second, as refugees in Pakistan and Iran, her family struggled on their own, in contravention of
the UN Convention and Protocol on Refugees to be taken care of on
account of their forced displacement. Malikka missed the opportunity
to go to school and was compelled to marry early to relieve her family
from poverty (one less mouth to feed). Third, her migration to Canada
was prompted by the educational needs of her daughter, causing her to
separate from her husband.

When Malikka migrated to Canada, she sought to unite her family
(to mend her split role of mother and wife) for which purpose she undertook waged work. She encountered racialized barriers and was compelled to take on low-paid and privatized work without fringe benefits.
She reached a point in her life whereby she was hospitalized:

> Because I was held in the [section for the] mentally disordered, the Minis-
> try of Children decided that I was not capable of taking care of my daugh-
> ter. So they took her to a Canadian woman's house where there was another
> girl as well.

Malikka explained that her daughter, Rehana, was placed in an alien
environment. She could not eat, and she found it difficult to adjust to
the rigid schedule:

> They ate breakfast early in the morning and dinner early in the evening.
> Eight o'clock was her bedtime. Rehana cried a lot, and she did not eat much.
> I used to talk to her every night. The lady [her foster mother] complained.

The ministry informed Malikka that she could only talk to Rehana once
a week to spare her the trauma of separation. Malikka recalled her and
her daughter's treatment at the hands of the police:

> My doctor had called the police. He thought I was not capable of looking
> after Rehana. The police believed that I was dangerous. So they wanted to

take my daughter, [but] she would not let me go. And they had to force me to leave my child. I am not happy with their behaviour towards my daughter. This experience [not excluding Rehana's encounter in the foster home] affected my daughter's mental health in a really bad way. She has nightmares.

Food has a presence, and it appears everywhere: on farms, on the shelves of produce stores, and more substantively, in kitchens, where it is transformed from a raw to a cooked stage for social consumption. Food can convey stories of lack reminiscent of the absence of meat in the households that I visited in Afghanistan. Food scarcity translates into hunger. There is also a reverse situation of the loss of appetite owing to extreme stress as has been the case with Rehana and Malikka. This silent script contains a powerful message of naming and remembering through the mirror image of not being able to eat despite the availability of food. It is through this minimal narrative that Malikka "inadvertently create[s] an autobiographical text" to use Kadar's words (2005, 99). It is worth reflecting on what Kadar has to say:

There is a need to question the restrictions we have used to exclude the voices of the deeply wounded, the refugee, and the survivor. The feature that autobiographical texts hold in common is the remembering of significant events in the writer's life, whether covertly or directly, whether seamlessly or in interrupted fragments. In minimal narratives, there is no opportunity for a "seamless I" to evolve and develop her character, but there is an opportunity for us in the current period to apprehend significant events in the writer's [narrator's] life, or in her community's life during inestimable hardship. (100)

It is in this vein that I continue with Malikka's narrative. She talked about how "both I and my daughter could not eat much. I could not swallow food knowing her condition. She [Rehana] told me that she did not eat much. She did not like the food and she was upset." This script requires politicized understanding. Food is ubiquitous; it is forever present in our lives at different times as we go about our business at home, in the workplace, and also during ritual ceremonies and rites of passage. Food is through and through social, and it also has an important sacred and cosmic component. In short, it is through food that we relate to the world, socially, spiritually, and materially. Malikka and Rehana did not consume food in the holistic sense (materially and socially) not because of its lack, in this case, but because it could not provide social nurturance. Malikka's stay in the hospital and her daughter's stay in the foster home encapsulate the violence of war (*khashonat jangi*) that Malikka has been subject to since her childhood. Moving around and living a harsh life in the second country of migration and also in Canada may be read in the context of food as a central component. We sustain our families and our communities through material and social nourishment (my summation of women's words). I am reminded of Kirmayer's observation that the failure of our imagination does not allow us to capture what is left unsaid in narrative accounts. And this failure, he argues, can lead to psychopathological interpretations that will reduce "the meaning of the patient's story to a series of signs or indices of illness and may foreclose the search for any larger narrative of coherence" (2003, 168).

Zulfikar has obtained the immigration visa and the family is reunited. Malikka says that she is not happy in the marriage: "not because of anything else. I just do not like him. It was a forced marriage owing to circumstances." Her frustration is expressed through food: "I do not cook Afghan food that much. I was not introduced to it. We like Iranian food, but I do not feel like cooking. I buy a lot of tinned stuff from the supermarket." A lifetime of pain caused by violence in war, along with structural insensitivity experienced in Canada, is expressed through the medium of food.

Malikka worries about her family members (siblings) who still reside in Afghanistan and Iran. She has learned from regular contact with her family that they struggle for food: "They do not have enough to eat. There are times when they have to live on naan and chai just as my family did." Malikka feels frustrated that she is not able to send money to them because she does not have enough for her own family. My research assistant, Golnaz, and I had planned to see Malikka one more time. However, this did not happen as she was hospitalized for depression.

In the above account, I have shown how food/foodscapes can exist as a silent script that needs to be read in a sociopolitical context. This means reading between the lines. The language of silence is not an unusual phenomenon. Disenfranchised people resort to this medium of communication, as the one means through which they convey the message of social suffering and harm. Ross (2003) calls for a new language of social suffering, "one that admits the integrity of silence" (165). Foodscapes constitute one means through which violence in the inner recesses of life can be made knowable and remembered. Food evokes memories integral to which are social and sacred dimensions. Food is not and never has been a discrete entity, as anthropologists have long observed. It is in this context that I have presented Malikka's narrative.

Remembering the Death of a Son (Pesar)

My name is Farida Ali, [and] I am thirty-one years old. I was two years old when I left Afghanistan. I am not sure what happened or the reasons why we left Afghanistan and went to Iran. I lived in Iran for twenty-seven years. When I was nine, my mother passed away. Life issues and problems were so many; I had to take care of my little brother, who was only six months old at that time. I got married when I was thirteen. It was a forced marriage, and I married my cousin, the son of my father's brother. Soon after our marriage, I got pregnant and gave birth to my first child, and because of my child I stayed in the relationship. I experienced many hard times in my life, in Iran. I only studied until grade four, when my mother passed away. [After that] I had to take care of my siblings: one of them was two, and the other one was six months old. After my marriage, when I gave birth to my second child, he got cancer at the age of eight. It was not cancer from the beginning, it was a skin fungus, but the doctors did not realize this issue and could not solve his problems, so his skin got really infected and he finally got blood cancer. He was hospitalized for four years, and I was with him almost twenty-four hours [a day]. I was in debt for about $20,000 [US], but yet, my son was not cured ... We sent my son's dead body to the UN to show them that they did nothing for my kid. We had waited for four years, for the UN to send us abroad and [to have] his illness cured. When the UN saw his dead body, they said, "We did not do anything for him, but we will help you to go abroad." Exactly at the same time that my son was hospitalized for cancer, my father got cancer as well, [but] he was in another hospital. My father was very young, only fifty-one. Forty days after my son's death, my father also passed away. It was really hard, [with] many life disasters. I had a sixteen-year-old sister at the time, and all my brothers and sisters were [left] alone.

The thread that binds Farida's narrative is remembering lifelong displacement climaxed in the death (*marg*) of her son. She was only two years old when her family was compelled to leave Afghanistan for Iran at the time of the Soviet invasion. She lost her childhood at the age of nine, as she had to take care of her two young brothers following the death of her mother. Then, at the age of thirteen, she was married to her cousin for reasons of poverty. She gave birth to four children. Her second son, Rizwan, fell sick at the age of eight and was hospitalized for a period of four years; his illness became worse because of misdiagnoses. The doctors advised her to take Rizwan abroad (to a western country) for treatment, and she approached the United Nations to facilitate this process. But, because of the delay in processing his case, Rizwan passed away.

Other than remembering the death of her son, Farida recalled the painful experience of not having food for the family:

> We all put up with the problems. You will not believe me if I tell you at that point [Rizwan's hospitalization], I had no money to buy food for my kids. I was not even able to buy cooking oil. My kids had nothing to eat. Having a kid hospitalized for four years is very expensive for his family. Each week, we had to pay 25,000 tomans (US$25) for his injections.

Farida received assistance from the United Nations, and an Iranian doctor brought lunch and dinner for Rizwan for a period of three months. Other than going hungry, the family took turns being with Rizwan on a rotating basis: "I would stay with him for fifteen days, my husband stayed with him for fifteen days, and my oldest son [Suleiman] stayed with his brother for fifteen days."

Farida feels betrayed. She believes that the United Nations could have brought Rizwan to Canada and saved his life: "UN did not do anything. My son could have been saved. Then he would be with us. I lost my son and after two months, my father passed away." She repeated: "UN did not do anything for my son. They could have saved him. I cannot forget that. Rizwan could have been saved. When we came to Canada, I cried a lot." The pain of dealing with a situation of illness and going hungry has not gone away. Kirmayer's observation rings true: "Nor does the violence endured by the refugees end with migration; it is embedded in the structures of most receiving societies" (2003, 181; cf. Silove et al. 2000). It is to this point of embedded violence that I now turn.

For Farida, Rizwan's memory is intertwined with that of Suleiman. Farida recalled the sacrifices he made in taking care of his brother: "He was only thirteen at the time. He suffered a lot." She recalled that he had to give up schooling, and then upon the family's migration to Canada, he was subject to bullying. His jaw was broken twice due to fights:

> The Canadian kids hit him, and he hit back. They operated on his jaw twice and we had to attend many court sessions. I told the court, "We had many problems in Iran. Not that Iranians treated us badly, it was life events. I lost my mother, my son, and my father. I did not feel my mother's death because

I was very young. But my father's death was really hard on me and so was the
death of my baby son."

Farida echoes what Kirmayer (2003) refers to as "narrative coherence."
In the court, she told the judge the whole story of the suffering caused by
the violence of war. The question is: Can the judge, and by extension the
reader, make a connection between her narrative linking Canada (*here*)
and Afghanistan/Iran (*there*) based on one particular scene of bullying?
Our inability to make this connection, Kirmayer argues, leads to the failure of imagination with disastrous consequences, as we are unable to
understand how violence rips apart "the world of everyday routine, community order and family roots" (169; also see Kirmayer 2002; Kirmayer
and Corin 1998)..

Farida observed:

> You know he [Rizwan] was very different and unique compared to my
> other children and the kids of his own age. He was very good looking and
> he used to talk very sweet. All the doctors and nurses loved him. They all
> thought that it was not fair for him not to get well. He passed away on the
> thirteenth day of Nouroz [New Year]. This will be the fourth year. They
> called me [in the] early morning and told me to come quickly as my son
> was asking for me. When I arrived at the hospital he told me, "I really
> missed you." He placed his head between my arms and exactly at that mo-
> ment he passed away.

She cried as she finished the story of her son's passing.

My reading of the above account suggests two points. First, I consider
Farida's memorization of her son's last moments as a performative act
requiring a dialogical engagement with an audience/the readers. Her
inclusion of the doctors and nurses as loving caregivers suggests this.
Waterson (2007) observes that individual memories must be transmitted
to make them social. In other words, Farida creates a wider expanse for
remembering her son. Second, as Phelps (2004, 69) explains:

> Stories enable citizens within a country to understand each other in ways
> that might otherwise not be possible. In countries that are deeply divided
> culturally, economically, politically, and otherwise, the sharing of personal
> narratives may be the only means by which such diverse people can recog-
> nize the humanity of the other. An experience of pain or the loss of a loved
> one crosses deep divides, and stories of pain and loss can bridge gaps in
> experience and lead to empathetic understanding.

Farida remembers her son every day, and commemorates his life during Nouroz, highlighting the aspect of food: "How else can I remember my son. He loved Nouroz when we had a special meal of fish. He passed away during this time (on the thirteenth day). Whatever I prepare on this day, it is for him." This is a bittersweet memory. Passing away on a special day like Nouroz means that he is remembered more widely as relatives and friends come together and share food. Farida's colleague Adila provided the following profile of Nouroz:

> For Nouroz every year, we make *kolooche* (a special kind of pastry) and other pastries at home. We buy fruit and nuts from the stores and also make the traditional rice and fish dinner at home. We go visit old friends, like we used to in Iran [second country of migration]. People also come to our place to visit us. For Sizdah bedar [the thirteenth day of the New Year], we all go out to a place of nature with other Afghan families. Each family brings food. We all get together in a park and have food together.

Four years have passed since Rizwan's death. Farida related, "Not a day goes by when I do not remember him. I pray for his soul. When I cook during Nouroz, I feel his presence. I feel that he is not dead. He is present in the celebration." This scenario contrasts with her eldest son, Suleiman, and his experience with food and social life. Suleiman has difficulties speaking and eating because of the jaw injury which doctors have not been able to completely repair. He makes funny noises while sitting with other people. When I asked him the reason, he said, "I cannot breathe normally. I have to do this to breathe. Sometimes I have to hold on to my jaw for breathing." Farida explained that he goes to McDonald's for meals, where he can remain anonymous. The irony of the dead son's remembrance during Nouroz festivities (a social and communal event), and the living son's exclusion from the social world of the food requires emphasis and calls for reflection against forgetting. Farida's story provides another illustrative example of violence in the inner recesses of life revealed through ambiguity (inclusion/exclusion) surrounding food.

The Food Bank

Food banks are synonymous with refugees and the working poor. They are set up in places where this constituency resides. The stated goal is to provide food to the needy. Comments made by service providers include: "They help the needy." "It makes it possible for the children to have enough food so that they do not go hungry." "Giving away food prevents wastage."

My observations at three sites in Valley View and its vicinity, suggest the following. First, the term "food" is understood in a restricted sense. Its distribution is governed by what is available from the corporations, what has expired, and what is in reality inexpensive high-carbohydrate stuff. A popular item is bread and its variations, such as muffins, bagels, and doughnuts. Furthermore, the social and symbolic aspects integral to food are not addressed, as food is translated, in this case, into satiation of hunger. Reducing food to this level undoubtedly compromises what it means to be a social being. Food is one means through which we nurture our sociality. Second, it is important to ask how we arrived at a situation whereby we accept that it is appropriate to provide low nutritional food to the needy, including the children. Does this not also compromise their humanity? This point needs emphasis in the light of the service provider's general understanding: give it to them rather than throwing it in the garbage.

Dehumanization has, indeed, become the norm at the time when food is distributed at the food banks. To begin with, there is a clear-cut divide between the providers and the recipients. Positioning themselves as benefactors, the providers establish the procedures; feedback is not sought from the recipients. The recipients are expected to make two trips to the site of distribution. The first trip is for registration, whereby a number is given to each individual along with the day and the time when they should pick up the food (mostly bread, complemented with dented or about-to-expire tinned or packaged items). Food is picked up during the second trip. It can be noted here that the registration method itself is practical: it saves time, as the recipients do not have to line up, and it helps the providers to determine the amount of food to be given to each family based on its size. Those who have not registered do not get any food unless there is some left over. Although the registration process has practical elements, the issue is that the providers, most of whom are volunteers, have the power: it is their system, and their way of doing things that privilege them, notwithstanding the fact that their ranks may also include established newcomers from war-torn countries.

The exercise of power by the providers is evident at the time when the food is distributed. The registered recipients, most of whom are women by themselves or with children seated in strollers, are expected to sit outside until the doors open, around 9:00 a.m. Then eight to ten people are admitted into the room at a time. Each person goes around the room stating their preference for the kind of bread they desire. To give an example, there are loaves of bread (brown and white), buns, doughnuts, bagels, and at times, muffins – all of which are near their expiration dates. Dented or about-to-expire tinned or packaged food is also distributed. One area where caution is exercised is that the food that includes lard as an ingredient is not given to the Muslims. Other than asking the recipients to choose the kind of bread preferred, there is no interaction between providers and recipients. In fact, there is some amount of policing, with the providers ensuring that no one takes food twice.

Of interest were some comments made by the providers during my visits. Once, there was a bag of muffins, sticky and squashed. A recipient put her hand out to pick up a few. The provider commented, "She is not supposed to touch them." Fifteen minutes later, the supervisor put the same muffins in the garbage, noting, "They are too sticky." Another woman with two children had forgotten to bring a bag. One of the providers informed me, "They are supposed to bring their own bags." On one occasion, a lot of bread was sent by a corporate organization (a giant food store). On this particular day, there were few recipients. Thus, those who came were given two large bags of bread. When I inquired as to what they would do with so much old bread, one of the providers said, "They have a freezer." A second provider noted that "they have cars," in response to my question on how they would carry two bags. She added, "Nothing is enough for them. I know one man. He comes here to collect the food and then he goes to a second food bank." These comments, reiterated in particular contexts are derogatory. They show how little the providers know about the wounds that each person bears, as she or he walks into the room to collect food that no one else wants. In this process of omission, the providers miss what Jackson (2006) considers as the social act of storytelling: "They bind people together in terms of meanings that are collectively hammered out. It is this sharing in the reliving of tragedy, this sense of communing in a common loss, that gives stories their power, not to forgive or redeem the past but to unite the living in the simple affirmation that they exist, that they have survived" (103).

There is another aspect to the food bank that requires comment. During the waiting period and after collecting food, the women get together and engage in animated conversation using their language with their fellow countrywomen. I have not been privy to their conversations. I gathered from research participants that their talk covers a range of topics from childrearing to opportunities in their country of settlement. Issues of racism and discrimination are also discussed. And in the process, the women engage in memory work recalling their lives as they had known them back home, and exchanging news on current developments in their countries of origin. The process of reliving the moments of displacement and (re)placement constitutes a critique of the "sanitized and distorted version of what they had suffered" (Douglass and Vogler 2003, 7): "In this respect, survivor witnesses of traumatic events do not provide knowledge or information in the usual sense; they are themselves the evidence, the knowledge that we receive from their existence as survivors" (38).

And their existence entails initiatives revealed in the way in which the women use the bread from the food bank. The participants identified three uses. First, after taking out what they will need themselves, the women distribute the bread to their peers and members of their extended family. The distribution does not take place as a discrete activity. While making a trip to the house of a peer or relative or vice versa, the women have chai over which they exchange stories and information of value to them. The women also exchange ideas on creative uses of bread to make it less stale. Examples include serving bread with fish or with homemade tomato sauce. The bread is also sometimes eaten toasted with butter and jam – "the Canadian way," as one woman expressed it. The significance of these activities comes to light as it can "provide space for recalling the past as they knew it, and a sharing of memories that can shed a different light on individual experiences furthers, and helps overcome feelings of victimization" (Hua 2005, 192).

It is within the space of service provision such as the food bank that the women bring up concerns of everyday life. Khadija cited an incident on curry and cigarettes. It is worth quoting her at length as she captures the spirit of the information that is exchanged outside the structure of the system, or over chai, consumed, for example, in the process of redistributing bread to peers and family members:

> People do not speak to immigrants the way they speak with native English speakers. The BC Housing [Corporation] does not value us as human beings. The less English you speak the louder they scream when they talk to you. If you act for your rights, they threaten to kick you out. When my white neighbour complained of the smell of the curry cooked by her Indian neighbour, she was treated with contempt. And so was I when I complained of the smell of cigarettes from the house behind us. My son has asthma. The manager told me, "This is Canada. This is how it works here. People have the right to smoke in their own homes." I could feel that the manager

thought that I am a troublemaker. "Be quiet or leave" is the message she was giving me.

The exchange of such stories, no doubt, makes one realize one is not alone. And shared oppression contains a political edge, especially when it is linked with memory work: "Memory is an act of remembrance that can create new understandings of both the past and the present" (Agnew 2005, 8). Rahima echoes this point: "I am not alone. If bad treatment is a problem for everyone, we need to do something about it. Maybe we should learn to speak up to protect our rights."

In the process of redistributing the extra bread within their social circles, the women give a new meaning to the food bank; they infuse it with social meaning woven into a political project of remembering, as noted earlier. Khadija expressed it this way:

Without these chats and reminiscences, I would feel great *khallah* (emptiness). Without talking to people who belong to the same past, there is nothing to invigorate my mind. Before I reconnected with my friends, my mind felt paralyzed (*falj*).

I am not suggesting that the women only connect through the spaces they create in the process of receiving services. Being able to create their own space in their country of settlement testifies to the power of food and memory work that the women articulate *here* and *there*. Here and there are sites that are connected, territorially, culturally, socially, and through the planet earth that we occupy as persons; politically constructed boundaries keep them apart.

Conclusion
Towards an Engaged Anthropology

Evoking the Attention of a Listening Audience

The women (*zanaan*) have spoken through the pages of this book using the construct of memory where the past (*gozashta*) is rendered present (*haal*), generating a dialogical narrative.[1] When people remember, they do so for an imagined audience; their recall of events is meant to create for a listener a feeling of being there. Exemplifying family and kinship,[2] the women in my study remembered knowing full well that their suffering has not been acknowledged by the world, a point of viewed confirmed by Daulatzai (2006, 306) and Waterson: "The failure of the rest of the world to intervene leaves some survivors, long after a return to 'normal' life, with a sense of being forever unjustly excluded from the human community" (2007, 62).

Stories provide flesh and bones to what may otherwise be intangible expressions of pain and suffering. The women know this, and they made many references to how "people do not know our stories (*qesa haa*) and what we have gone through." They are clearly aware that others "cannot imagine how wars have destroyed (*kharaab kardan*) our lives." It is through memorialized narratives that they relived disruptive events imprinted in their everyday lives (*zindagi rozmara*): the Soviet invasion, the civil war, the rise of the Taliban, and the US-led invasion and occupation of Afghanistan post-9/11.[3] Razia recounted:

> I lost my husband during the mujahideen war. Now I have to depend on my brother to support me. Do you know what it means to be helpless (*bechaara*) and to live a life filled with *moshkelil* (difficulties)? I have no children (*atfaal*). He [my husband] died before we could have children.

We can only imagine what life would be like for a young war widow who has no home or financial security of her own. In Valley View (Burnaby, BC), Sabrina relayed how her marriage almost broke up due to the difficulties they faced in Canada:

> My husband [Rahim] wanted to go back to Pakistan where he had started a small business. I told him, "We cannot go back. We have to look at the future (*ayenda*) of our children. They will get an education here." Rahim was known in Pakistan. People (other Afghans) called him, and asked for his advice. Here, in Canada, he is nobody. He delivers pizza. He does not feel that he is important.[4] There was a lot of conflict and tension. He almost left me.

The depth of violence contained in Sabrina's story is captured by Jackson: "Though violence may or may not entail physical harm, we may conclude that a person's humanity is violated whenever his or her status as a subject is reduced *against his or her will* to mere objectivity, for this implies that he or she no longer exists in any active relationship to others, but solely in the passive relationship to himself or herself" (2006, 45, original emphasis; cf. Hastrup 2003, 312)

Through multiple examples related individually in the presence of other Afghan women, the women brought into relief the disruptive effects of violence.[5] The ethnographic data presented in this book require close attention to questions such as: What is it like not to be able to attend the funeral of a close relative because of a security threat? What is it like when festive occasions are equated with ordinary days as families do not have the means to celebrate them? What is it like if you cannot send your children to school because they have to earn one or two dollars a day for bread? What is it like not to have access to a health facility because of distance, or because you do not have money for transport? What is it like to have your support system of kin and kith disrupted by protracted conflict? What is it like for a widow to take care of four to six children? What is it like to come to a new country and encounter racism and social exclusion, as opposed to systemic and sustained support? These are the realities resulting from the violence of war.

I am reminded of the two interrelated questions posed by Das and Kleinman (2001, 4): "How does one shape a future in which the collective experience of violence and terror can find recognition in the narratives of larger entities such as the nation and the state? And at the level of interpersonal relations, how does one contain and seal off the violence that might poison the life of future generations?."[6] My response to the first question posed above is shaped by scholarship on narrativized memories.[7] People remember through stories to elicit the attention of a larger audience (readers, researchers, and stakeholders). Here, as Fassin (2007) reminds us, the mediating role of the anthropologist is crucial. Containing and sealing off violence, stated in the second question, requires space for engagement – space that the women have created through memory work that takes us into the inner recesses of their lives. To summarize their important collective message – "Look, these are the effects of violence. Violence does not spare anyone, you or me" – is reminiscent of Butler's observation that precariousness must be recognized "as a shared condition of human life" (2009, 13). It is on these grounds that she makes the argument that "there ought to be a more inclusive and egalitarian way of recognizing precariousness and this should take form as concrete social policy regarding such issues as shelter, work, food, medical care and legal status" (13). A major challenge here is to interrogate what appears to be ordinary and normalized.

Culinary performance/foodscapes was also a means through which women engaged in memory work. Performance – everyday enactment of procuring, preparing, and consuming food, in this case – speaks louder than words. What does it mean when women prepare meals with minimal ingredients day in and day out? How do we acknowledge the presence of a vegetable patch, a shadow of one's former garden? The larger script here is that of the long-lasting impact of violence entrenched in areas that are barely noticed. How do we explain the situation of women struggling to put together a meal with its sociosymbolic significance in her home country (war-ravaged) as well as in the country of her settlement (indifferent to the plight of refugees).

Through their memories, the women convey the message: the destruction wrought by violence is not confined to one place. While remembering for Afghanistan they also remember for the world – mindful of the scars and the wounds embedded in their *mamlakat* (country). Oftentimes, my participants pointed to the white flags (*beragh safed*) on the roadside stating: "People are buried here. They gave their lives to protect our country." Other statements included: "Have you seen the King's palace? It is in ruins (*kharabah*). Did you see those burned buildings? They were part of our heritage. Now you cannot recognize them." The women remembered other sites such as the bazaars, the health clinics, schools, and parks that are in ruins today. They are aware of the reconstruction projects around their city, such as supermarkets, Western-style malls, and apartment complexes, but they felt that these did not serve them. In the words of one woman, "They are for the foreigners. We get what is left over." The malls and the supermarkets are primarily used by the expatriates and the minority population of middle-class Afghan families. Their sentiments echo Todeschini's (2001) work on the bombed women of Japan (Hiroshima and Nagasaki). Using the metaphor of "the bomb in the womb," these women bring into relief the destructive power of the nuclear bomb for the human race. The women of Afghanistan have taken the first step in showing that war undermines our sense of personhood embedded in networks of social and kinship ties. In doing so, they leave us with the question: What is our responsibility as researchers and listeners? In speaking for anthropologists, Fassin (2007) suggests that we could serve to "make known what had been unknown until then ... a truth might be told that would otherwise disappear forever" (20). However, to make known the everyday enactment of violence is not free of dilemmas. Consider the following examples.

In exploring the question of accountability, Scheper-Hughes (1992) notes that placing undue attention on the multiple ways in which the peasants in Brazil "survive in the cracks and crevices of daily life" renders opaque "the horrifying scene of the savagery of scarcity and the brutality of police terror" (508). An exclusive focus on resistance leads to a situation where the oppressed are held responsible "for their collusions, collaborations, rationalizations, false consciousness, and more than occasional paralyses of will" (533). On the other hand, documentation of the larger scene through which acts of brutality and terror are exercised on the "helpless" peasants victimizes them and misses out the multiple ways in which they exercise agency and assert their autonomy. Scheper-Hughes suggests that researchers take a middle-ground position in order to negotiate the dilemma, where resistance is not unduly romanticized and where suffering does not translate into lack of agency.

Adopting the role of an advocate for the poor and the oppressed, Farmer (2003) puts forward the concept of structural violence that he defines as a lack of opportunities for basic rights of employment, decent housing, and access to education and health care. Our responsibility as anthropologists is to explain this lack in relation to how global capitalism and neoliberalism translate into local scenarios. Unless we explore the relationship between social injustice and suffering, Farmer argues, we will end up managing social inequality rather than addressing it. Kleinman et al. (1997) and Das and Kleinman (2001) focus on delineating multilayered social contexts. At one level, they note, we should work towards identifying the social, economic, and political factors that cause suffering; yet, at another level, we need to map the ways in which these factors, in the form of ideology and practice, become embedded in local institutions. Designed to alleviate suffering, institutional responses, in fact, accentuate it. The study of social suffering, therefore, must contain a study of society's silence towards it.

In short, the above authors urge the reader to take into account local idioms of dismay and grief in the wake of powerful bureaucratic forces that normalize suffering for political purposes. The intention here is to expose appropriation of suffering by institutions that reify and fragment it and cast a veil of misrecognition onto what is essentially whole. Otherwise, "the vicious spiral of political violence, causing forced uprooting, migration, deep trauma to families and communities ... spins out of control across a bureaucratic landscape of health, social welfare and legal agencies" (Kleinman et al. 1997, x). The issue is that society conspires to "hide from itself how much suffering is imposed upon individuals as a price for belonging; and the social sciences may be in danger of mimicking society's silence towards this suffering" (Das 2003, 563). Acknowledging violence and social suffering is challenging because the workings of sociopolitical forces are not easily identifiable. In such a situation, the burden of suffering as well as recovery is placed on the individual severed from social life. It is for this reason that we need to recognize that suffering is not exclusively a product of the "contingencies of life but has to be conceptualized as actively produced and even rationally administered by institutions of the state" (566).

The above works bring to light the tension between on-the-ground realities (the local) and the broader political context – the source of suffering and oppression. The scholarly literature on violence and suffering remains polarized, as substantively we have not been able resolve the gap between the geopolitical forces and their impact on the quotidian realities: the presence of violence in the inner recesses of life. Scheper-Hughes' middle-ground approach is viable insofar as it provides a balanced perspective. Nevertheless, it suggests a division of labour, where the experts take care of the political perspective while the research participants provide the raw data. In this approach, the participants are not considered to be "experts" on the political economy. Addressing this Cartesian tension, some scholars (Dossa 2004, 2009; Collins 2000; Moore 1996, 2000) suggest that we must recognize our research participants as producers of knowledge in their own right. This knowledge may not be exclusively expressed in the language of the dominant society where the experience of pain and suffering is diluted and silenced. Alternative forms of expression are of interest as they make it possible for the research participants to undertake multiple tasks: to critique the larger system in their own terms, to establish the link between the individual body and the body politic, and to remake their worlds in relation to the larger society and not within discrete and marginalized spaces. It is in this context that I have presented women's memory work. The women in this study speak to the larger issue of harm and destruction caused by violence in war; it is through them that Afghanistan remembers. In short, a way out of the dilemma of mapping the political economy of violence without subduing human agency is to identify alternative forms of expression deployed by the interlocutors. This provides an entry point into engaged anthropology.

Engaged Anthropology

Engaged anthropology requires us to undertake multiple tasks. At one level, it calls upon the practitioners of the discipline to uncover systems of exclusion brought to light in the context of everyday life.[8] By encapsulating the workings of such a system, everyday life reveals the multiple ways in which people survive within spaces of devastation. Citing Ndebele (1994, 55), Ross states, "We must contend with the fact that even under the most oppressive conditions, people are always trying and struggling to maintain a semblance of normal social order" (2003, 140–1). This task, I argue, requires that we pay attention to how our interlocutors voice their experiences of exclusion and recovery through the deployment of particular genres/constructs. Depending on the historical, social, and political trajectories of their lives, alternative genres of expression may include social space (Low 2011), the language of silence (Ross 2003), the language of everyday life (Das 2007; Dossa 2009), social memory (Degnen 2005), and history in the flesh (Fassin 2007).

Disenfranchised people's usage of alternative constructs may be explained in relation to limitations of language and public space where only certain kinds of experiences are validated – namely, those that do not question the sociopolitical system. Language does not exclusively contain the suffering and particular experiences of violence in war. In her work on the Truth and Reconciliation Commission in South Africa, for example, Ross (2003) makes the point that public institutions tend to focus on the expressible and the bodily violations "at the expense of the broader understanding of apartheid and its consequences" (162).

The gendered dimension is particularly noteworthy as women's experiences are homogenized and medicalized by the state, limiting the avenues through which they can articulate their concerns. Furthermore, language does not lend itself to capturing the complex experiences of pain and suffering in time and space. It is in this context that Ross calls for a new language of violence that could include silence (but also memory work) as "it marks particular kinds of knowing" (49). The appeal of memory work, I suggest, lies in its capacity to capture the quotidian realities of life – realities that are otherwise taken to be fixed and normalized.

Having established that people on the social margins use alternative means of expression, our responsibility as readers and listeners is to move into the spaces created by our participants so that we can acquire a palpable understanding of the work of violence in the inner recesses of life to the extent that this is possible. It is in this light that Degnen (2005) makes the comment: "Within only a few months of starting fieldwork, I had already been well-schooled in various *landmarks of my research participants'* lives, landmarks that had been repeated to me many times already and which were to continue to figure powerfully in my fieldwork experiences" (737; emphasis added).

Narrative scholars have argued that, once we hear stories, we should stay with them rather than move on; in other words, we should acknowledge and recognize people's pain as opposed to dismissing it. It is in this spirit, I argue, that we should "dwell" in the spaces that our interlocutors create so as to acquire a humane understanding of their experiences. This, I argue, should form the core of engaged anthropology. This stance does not eradicate the goal of unravelling systemic injustice and inequality; it means recognizing that our interlocutors' experiences of violence in war resonate with our own given the deeper and broader understanding of violence (as physical, structural, epistemological, and normalized in the deeper recesses of life). Not discounting sociocultural and historical differences, we as human beings are not immune to suffering and pain.

Das (1996) has observed that "denial of the other's pain is not about the failings of the intellect but the failings of the spirit. In the registrar of the imaginary, the pain of the other not only asks for a home in language but also seeks a home in the body" (88; cf. Ross 2003, 49; also see Zarowsky 2004). I would like to extend this observation to include the space of imagination where we recognize our shared humanity – a point that I would not dismiss as idealistic given the existence of sociopolitical and economic inequalities globally, and on a scale that is vast. As Butler has expressed it, "Where life stands no chance of flourishing, there one must attend to ameliorating the negative condition of life" (2009, 23). I believe that we need to take a step in the direction of reducing these inequalities that have created a world where the global South bears the brunt of suffering. The space of imagination constitutes an alternative space for dialogue and conversation.

Through the pages of this book, I have argued that the violence of war entrenched in the inner recesses of life becomes knowable through the alternative construct of gendered memory work. Our understanding of this violence requires a leap of imagination through which we move into the space created by our interlocutors. It is within this shared space – a slippery slope in an unequal world – that we can recognize the disastrous effects of violence globally, a recognition that could form part of engaged anthropology. The importance of this engagement can be appreciated by the fact that violence destroys the centre of social life and compromises our humanity.

As this manuscript goes to the press, Afghan President Hamid Karzai has spoken. In a nationally televised speech (7 Oct. 2013), he stated that NATO has "caused Afghanistan a lot of suffering, a lot of loss of life, and no gains because the country is not secure" (http://www.bbc.co.uk/news/world). His words connote the completion of a circle. In 2001, NATO toppled the Taliban regime with the expressed intent of bringing peace and security to Afghanistan along with securing the rights of women. This has not happened. Karzai now intends to shake hands with the Taliban leaving the women in a precarious position. Women's oppressors will be back in power after thirteen years of foreign occupation of the country – an occupation that has been no less than a brutal enactment of violence within the inner recesses of life as I have shown in this book. The project of nation building will once again take place through the sacrifice of women rupturing their lives and their kith and kinship ties. It is my hope that the world will acknowledge this gendered script unfolding in war-ravaged countries globally.

The story continues (*Quessa edama darad*).

Appendix

Name	Age	Residence	No. of Children	Education	Marital Status	Occupation
Adila	30s	Canada	4	Grade 12	Married	Service worker
Ama	60s	Afghanistan	6	None	Widow	Grandmother
Ali	40s	Canada	5	Grade 12	Married	Produce store owner
Amina	40s	Canada	3	B.A.	Widow	Teacher
Bibi Gul	70s	Afghanistan	5	None	Widow	Grandmother
Dolat	40s	Canada	3	Grade 8	Married	Cashier
Fatima	30s	Afghanistan	4	Grade 12	Married	Service worker
Frema	40s	Afghanistan	5	Grade 8	Widow	Housewife
Farida	40s	Afghanistan	4	Grade 12	Married	Service worker
Hamida	50s	Afghanistan	3	None	Married	Cleaner
Hassan	40s	Canada	4	Grade 8	Married	Produce store owner
Jamila	40s	Afghanistan	4	Grade 5	Widow	Housewife
Khadija	40s	Afghanistan	6	Grade 6	Married	Housewife
Kulsum	40s	Afghanistan	5	Grade 6	Married	Housewife
Leila	40s	Afghanistan	5	Grade 8	Married	Housewife
Malikka	40s	Canada	3	Grade 8	Married	Housewife
Maryam	50s	Canada	4	Grade 4	Married	Housewife
Meena	60s	Canada	5	None	Married	Grandmother
Mehrun	30s	Afghanistan	3	Grade 12	Married	Housewife
Mehrunisha	40s	Afghanistan	3	Grade 3	Married	Housewife
Malikka	40s	Canada	2	Grade 7	Married	Housewife
Mah Puri	70s	Afghanistan	5	None	Widow	Grandmother
Nahila	30s	Canada	4	Grade 11	Married	Housewife
Nargis	40s	Canada	5	Grade 5	Married	Housewife
Naseem	30s	Canada	3	Grade 8	Married	Cashier

(Continued)

Name	Age	Residence	No. of Children	Education	Marital Status	Occupation
Nashrin	30s	Canada	4	Grade 11	Married	Housewife
Nazlin	30s	Afghanistan	3	Grade 11	Widow	Teacher
Razia	40s	Canada	3	Grade 11	Married	Cashier
Rehana	30s	Canada	3	Grade 11	Married	Cashier
Rehmet	40s	Canada	4	Grade 12	Married	Produce store owner
Rahima	40s	Canada	0	Grade 7	Unmarried	Casual
Roshan	50s	Afghanistan	3	Grade 7	Married	Housewife
Rashida	40s	Canada	5	Grade 7	Married	Cashier
Raqib	40s	Canada	4	Grade 6	Married	Casual
Samira	40s	Afghanistan	4	Grade 8	Widow	Housewife
Sadaf	50s	Canada	5	Grade 12	Widow	Service worker
Salima	40s	Canada	4	Grade 12	Married	Cashier
Shireen	40s	Canada	3	Grade 12	Married	Cashier
Siteza	40s	Afghanistan	4	Grade 8	Widow	Housewife
Shirooz	40s	Afghanistan	4	Grade 7	Married	Housewife
Tamiza	30s	Afghanistan	4	Grade 8	Married	Housewife
Zahra	40s	Canada	3	Grade 4	Widow	Housewife
Zarin	40s	Afghanistan	3	Grade 8	Married	Service worker

The above represent primary respondents only. This is an ethnographic study entailing conversations with dozens of women.

Housewife includes petty trade work from home (participants in Afghanistan).

Cashier refers to manual work; Afghan Canadian women preferred to use this term.

Service worker refers to fast-tracked training provided to Afghan women by international NGOs.

The study participants could not complete their education owing to disruption caused by wars.

Notes

1. Epistemology and Methodology

1 Acknowledging the importance of everyday and life, Das (2007) notes, "Words that lead lives outside the ordinary, become emptied of experience, lose touch with life" (6). It is in this vein that I have placed emphasis on everyday life; in many ways it represents the inner recesses where violence is enacted.

2 Fassin (2007) lays out the steps through which anthropologists can revisit the issue of social justice. First, he notes that we must move away from a state of "political anesthesia" to recognize the humanness of other people; second, we must acknowledge our shared destiny involving an understanding that "anthropology's Other is, ultimately, other people who are our contemporaries" (xii). Third, Fassin advocates historically based ethnography apprehended by local people with their complex relationships to the past and the present. In short, the path towards social justice is not simple and cannot be underestimated.

3 Feminist ethnographers have been at the forefront of highlighting the complex play of power in the field. In her seminal work, *Feminism and Anthropology*, Moore (1988) suggests the framework of intersectionality to highlight the concept of power due to its focus on "how gender is structured and experienced through colonialism, through neo-imperialism and through the rise of capitalism" (10). Identifying the need to include Muslim and Middle Eastern women in the debates on politics and power in the field and beyond, anthropologist Abu-Lughod calls for interrogation of "the relationship between the constructs of 'East' and 'West' as they have shaped anticolonial nationalistic projects" (1998, 5).

4 For a comprehensive analysis, refer to *Nation-Building Unraveled: Aid, Peace and Justice in Afghanistan* (Donini, Niland, and Wermester 2004).

5 It is through our interlocutors that we learn how violence becomes entrenched in the inner recesses of life. Through them we come to know details of life that are otherwise dismissed as mundane. In her work, *Life and Words*, Das (2007) argues that it is in the recesses of the ordinary that we acquire an understanding of the ways in which violence is actualized.

6 Malinowski (1922), the founder of ethnographic research, put forward a layered method of "participant observations." This method entails gradual entry into the field so as to obtain a sense of place and knowledge of the people, including their everyday lives. I found this method to be helpful. Not only did I come to know the participants (women, service providers, professionals, and storekeepers) by hanging out, they also got used to my presence. For example, when I visited the community centre and the stores on Valley View, I was well received. Knowing what to say as a Muslim (greetings, inquiring on the well-being of families, discussion on topical issues) helped to establish a rapport complemented with informal conversations.

7 Todeschini's comments are insightful: "The public acknowledgement and appropriation of illness, loss, pain, and grief and the establishment of gender categories in connection with suffering, are profoundly political acts, which draw boundaries and determine 'appropriate' expression of suffering" (2001, 104). She presents, too, narratives of women in an attempt to reverse the process of appropriation. In this vein, the time span specified is necessary to capture moments of retraumatization and rebuilding of lives through memory work.

8 My focus on Afghan women has not freed me from the dilemma raised by Nagel (2005): How do we present a complicated reading of their lives so as not to suggest a homogeneous picture? According to Nagel, there is no way out of this dilemma. In my case, I felt the need to bring to the fore the violence of war impacting the lives of the women and their families while exercising caution to move away from a monolithic picture to the extent possible. A focus on memory work, narratives, and food – embedded in everyday life – allowed me to present a more complicated picture.

9 Also refer to Abu-Lughod (2002), Grima (1992), Khattak (2002), and Stabile and Kumar (2005). Calling for a more complex understanding of Afghan women's status, these authors call for an interrogation of the US-led trope of liberating the women.

10 Khan (2001) calls for a nuanced reading of Afghan women's narratives at home and in the diaspora. She suggests an analysis that historicizes the narratives so as to reverse "the reductive images of veiled Afghan women" (1).

I have drawn insights from her work, especially her argument on the politicized linkage between the West and the East.

11 In her work, *Diaspora, Memory and Identity*, Agnew (2005) notes, "The past is always with us, and it defines our present; it resonates in our voices, hovers over our silences, and explains how we came to be ourselves and to inhabit what we call 'our homes'" (3).

12 By way of promoting multilevel field research, Frank (2000) suggests a "methodology in action." Within this rubric, we can simultaneously address issues of power, engage in collaborative research, and ask pertinent political and social questions. It is in this vein that I have presented a framework where methodology and epistemology are intertwined.

2. Testimonial Narratives

1 In their work in *Remaking a World*, Das and Kleinman (2001) emphasize a vision of the polis that allows one "to speak for oneself politically – to be able to find a voice *in community with other voices*" (4; original emphasis). This is a gradual process that requires public acknowledgment of one's experiences of violence – the core theme of this book.

2 My choice to focus on two women is based on highlighting the singularity of lives, a notion that has been well received in anthropology, and in the literature on narratives. In her work, *Venus on Wheels*, Gelya Frank (2000) documents the life history of a woman with disabilities (Diane) over a period of twenty years. Rather than being a mere life story, Diane encapsulates societal issues such as her being part of the second wave of feminism in the United States.

3 Scholars on social memory have informed us that "before" is not a nostalgic image of the past; it serves a political purpose of critiquing the larger systems of power. People who remember give the message: "Look what our lives have been reduced to from a former state; we did not bring about this situation" (see Baines 2007; Bairner 2008; Bourguignon 2005; Crumley 2002; Sugiman 2004, 2009; Waterson 2007).

4 Afs50 (the Afghan currency) amounts to US$1.00. This discrepancy speaks to the US and Western hegemony. Lindisfarne (2008) defines this hegemony in the form of "the global economic and political system that serves the interests of members of an international ruling class" (25).

5 Western hegemony is "legitimized by government institutions of the rich countries of the North, and underwritten by the force of the American military machine" (Lindisfarne 2008, 25). The issue is that ending militarized violence in Afghanistan does not capture entrenched structural vulnerability.

6 Penetration of violence in the inner recesses of life disrupts family life, undermining traditional networks of support. In "The Family during Crisis in Afghanistan," Dupree (2004) documents the ways in which the traditional structures of family life were ruptured during different phases of the conflict. While we take into account the hierarchical structure of family life and gender dynamics, we must also pay attention to what kinds of support systems existed and how these operated or became dysfunctional in times of crisis (also refer to Kandiyoti 2005, 2007).

7 Food is taken as given except in times of crisis. But it is "noisy" and speaks louder than words (see Gvion 2006; Rosenberger 2007).

8 I would like to emphasize that this was a recurring theme. The women not only included their cohort in their narratives, but were aware of their shared oppression brought about by the violence of war. They shared each other's struggles as they went about performing everyday tasks carried out in a common yard or within the space of their respective neighbourhoods. They also engaged in reciprocal exchanges of food and services in kind, tapping into the tradition of mutual support and assistance.

9 This example highlights the value of remembering for one's cohort. Amina does not only engage in memory work on behalf of other widows; she reconfigures the meaning of widowhood.

10 For a comprehensive review of the politics of refugee return, refer to Turton and Marsden (2002).

11 Through her account on the quotidian realities of life, Amina shows how people survive on the margins of society. Survival is not reduced to mere consumption of food. It entails the multiple ways in which women and men carry on with their lives using cultural resources, such as starting the day with prayers, establishing daily routines, and fostering sociality.

12 It is evident that violence in war creates structural vulnerability that in itself has repercussions for family life. This is one reason why this form of violence must become knowable to the outside world.

13 I would like to validate the significance of narrative fragments. Related within the space of ethnographic conversations, they provide a trenchant critique of society by means of metaphors, words, and images.

3. Bearing Witness

1 It takes courage and energy to relay one's story of pain and suffering. When narrators share their stories, they do so with a purpose. Other than trying to make sense of their own lives as to how they arrived at the present situation, their intent is to create space for a listening community (see, e.g., Dossa 2009; Fassin 2007; Ong 1995).

2 None of the research participants came directly from Afghanistan. Two reasons can be attributed to this reality. First, many of the families had to leave Afghanistan overnight owing to immediate risk to their lives. Second, enduring more suffering in another country (largely Pakistan, Iran, and/or India) gave them "the passport" to migrate to Canada. As Malkki (1995) has observed, you have to adopt the label of suffering and victimized refugee to solicit the attention of international aid organizations.

3 The power of collective/testimonial speaking whereby a singular story captures the life worlds of others in a situation of shared suffering needs to be underscored. This mode of telling, as Waterson (2007) has noted, "generates its own meaning and demands a dialogical engagement with/by an audience" (51).

4 I have reiterated these points for emphasis and to provide a context.

5 Meena's reference to the invasion of Iraq in 2003 conveys the message of an ongoing enactment of violence, revealing how one incident can unleash forces that catch momentum.

6 They highlighted issues concerning job and career opportunities, housing, budget, racism, social alienation, children's education, sociality, access to health, and the practice of Islam. This is not a laundry list. Cumulatively, these issues contribute to stresses and tensions that people from war-ravaged countries should not be subjected to in their country of settlement. The women also talked about attempts to rebuild their lives and how they negotiate in-between spaces: the public and the private worlds, Canada and homeland, secularism and spirituality, everyday lives and institutional structures, and the young and the old; see Spitzer (2011) for a comprehensive overview on gender and migrant health in Canada. They worried about their families in Afghanistan and other parts of the global South knowing full well that they, too, struggle under the heavy weight of violence in the inner recesses of life, not acknowledged by the larger society.

4. The Fire of the Hearth Will Not Be Extinguished

1 Hastrup (2003) observes that language cannot capture the full experience of violence. Hypothetically, if this were possible, people's experiences of violence and suffering would be objectified. From this point of view, the mediums of memory and food are critical: they reveal the workings of violence within spaces that are not otherwise noticed, and hence, they remain socially invisible.

2 At the same time, we must find ways to connect local realities to national and global spaces. In this study, I have suggested two ways: (1) Ensure that we recognize the intricate linkages between the global South and the global

North in relation to a shared history; what happens over there (Afghanistan) is a function of the policy-based and "military" decisions over here (Canada). (2) As people who seek to valorize the experiential knowledge of research participants, anthropologists have an obligation to respond.

3 It is important to note the intricate process of recovery. Here the issue is not that of mere survival but of living with dignity. Accompanied by Rehmet (the service provider from Baraka), I visited the home of a widow, Amina. She lives in one room with her mother-in-law and her three children. When we entered the house/room, Amina had laid out naan (bread), potatoes, and water on a mat on the floor. Hoping that I would make a case for her to receive assistance, she wished to "show" how poor she was. She did not relay this situation to me verbally. Maybe it would have compromised her dignity; and perhaps she felt that words would not capture her suffering brought about by circumstances not of her making. As we were driving back to Baraka, Rehmet informed me that this is not how poor people live. Rehmet wanted to give me the cultural message that food is not laid out in a haphazard way, and that Amina would ensure that her children would first give the food to their grandmother before consuming it themselves. I observed that the women were experiencing tension as to whether they should present the face of poverty to obtain assistance in the wake of the destruction of their country's infrastructure, or present the face of dignity. I was impressed by the women's organizational skills. They have created a home for their families even if they live in one room. They had designated corners for cooking and for children to do their homework. At nighttime, a one-room house is converted into a bedroom, and in the daytime, it becomes a sitting room. This transformation takes place through the skilful use of mats – folded neatly during the day and opened up at night. Makeshift curtains are used to divide the room into two parts, maximizing the usage of space.

4 My observations in other districts (Shar-e-Naw, Kote Shangi, and Kate Parwan) revealed a similar pattern.

5 My driver always played Bollywood songs. When I asked him if he ever played Afghan songs, he said, "I was young when I went to Pakistan. I did not learn Afghan songs. I like Bollywood songs. It reminds me of my life in Pakistan." On another occasion, he talked of the harsh conditions that he and his family had to endure living in exile. This example reveals both loss (Afghan songs) and substituted gain (Bollywood songs), revealing the dynamics of remembering and forgetting, integral to memory work.

6 These observations apply to close-knit relationships not devoid of tensions and conflicts.

5. Foodscapes

1 The contradiction is not noticeable. The multicultural face of Canada is evident at Valley View. What remains hidden is that the people who walk down the streets have many stories to tell – stories of wars and conflicts in their countries of origin, and stories of indifference and racialization in their new homeland in Canada.

2 The women in my study were conscious that although they are able to purchase more food items – because as Zahra expressed it, "They are less expensive and you can get them on sale" – they are, nevertheless, high in carbohydrates, i.e., unhealthy. They expressed concern that their young children are acquiring a taste for these unhealthy and fast foods. Some of the women reported that owing to health education in schools, their children are leaning towards nutritious foods. Through their children, the women are learning how to be "healthy in Canada," as Shabnum stated it. At the same time, they are aware that healthy food costs more money.

3 This is an example of grassroots-level initiatives. Linking these to judicial and political bodies would make a difference in people's lives. Not allowing families to unite for the purpose of visiting is unjust, compounded in the situation of racial profiling that Muslims are subject to in large numbers post-9/11 (see Razack 2000; Razack et al. 2010).

4 In her recent book, *A Quiet Revolution*, Leila Ahmed (2011) provides a historical trajectory of the veil's resurgence from the Middle East to America. She links Muslim American women's nuanced practice of *hijab* (veiling and unveiling) to "Islamic 'feminist' activism" in the post 9/11 era (293). The Afghan women in Canada with whom I interacted were also engaged in this project generationally. Referring to the activist stance of her daughter, Rahima put it this way: "My daughter is the voice of the oppressed generation of Afghan, Muslim, and immigrant women." Note how Rahima expands the horizons of her own country to include Muslim and immigrant women. This move ushers a shift towards transnational feminist activism (see, e.g., Khan 2008).

5 The purchase of halal meat is not an issue in Afghanistan. Muslims place emphasis on the fact that the animals are subject to minimal pain when slaughtered in a certain way along with a prayer. Halal meat is a special item in Canada – super food stores rarely carry it. They would only do so if there were a market, and not for the reason of accommodating a racialized minority. It is at such junctures that we need to question the meaning of "multiculturalism" which, in essence, is meant to accommodate cultural minorities.

6 Women's (and men's) activism in everyday life is barely noticed. Yet, everyday life reveals the fault lines of the system and, at the same time, has the potential to effect change (see Dossa 2009).

7 The majority of the homes I visited had red rugs and carpets. Embedded within each rug or carpet were memories of displacement, migration, and resettlement. One scene stands out: the women often referred to how they would roll out carpets for family members taking shelter in their homes in Afghanistan or abroad. This hospitality was normatively reciprocal: "When we went to Peshawar (Pakistan), my uncle rolled out the carpets for us to sleep" (Nargis). Overall, the red carpets provided homelike decor not devoid of memories of the flight – "the escape story."

8 I am not suggesting that this is a typical profile. It is included to highlight thematic issues.

9 Note how women negotiate their citizenship rights. They are not given; they are brought forward contextually.

Conclusion: Towards an Engaged Anthropology

1 It is important to emphasize this point as the past can easily be reified. Its impact on the lives of the people, especially in situations of protracted conflict, needs public recognition if we are to address the issue of violence inflicted on ordinary citizens. See, e.g., Baines (2007), Barak (2007), Bourguignon (2005), Brand (2010), Crumley (2002).

2 I do not take women/gender to be a discrete social category. My research shows that women embody the pulse and the rhythm of familial and community life and, by extension, that of the country as a whole, including the diaspora.

3 These events and the link between them are not politicized (Daulatzai 2006; Dupree 1990, 2004; Ghafour 2007; Goodson 2001; Kandiyoti 2005, 2007; Khattak 2002; Rubin 2000, 2002).

4 It is not far-fetched to state that asylum seekers are not accorded substantive citizenship rights in Canada. The question that arises for consideration is: Why has the system not tapped into Rahim's business experience? There are countless examples on alternative ways of being.

5 Grima (1992) shows that gendered storytelling is a cultural phenomenon. Stories are related in groups and have a therapeutic function because of the popularity of sad (*gamm*) stories.

6 Narrativized memories: see, e.g., Kadar 2005; Lyons 2010; Ong 1995; Ross 2001, 2003; Sugiman 2004, 2009.

7 I have given central space to everyday life as it is pregnant with meaning. It reveals taken-for-granted quotidian realities that are barely noticed. Yet, their significance cannot be underestimated, as it is through these realities that we can identify the fault lines of the system and work towards progressive change.

References

Abu-Lughod, Lila, ed. 1998. *Remaking Women: Feminism and Modernity in the Middle East.* Princeton: Princeton University Press.

– 2002. "Do Muslim Women Really Need Saving? Anthropological Reflections on Cultural Relativism and Its Others." *American Anthropologist* 104 (3): 783–90. http://dx.doi.org/10.1525/aa.2002.104.3.783.

Adams, Bert N., and Mike Bristow. 1978. "The Politico-Economic Position of Ugandan Asians in the Colonial and Independent Eras." *Journal of Asian and African Studies* 13 (3–4): 151–66. http://dx.doi.org/10.1177/002190967801300301.

– 1979. "Ugandan Asian Expulsion Experiences: Rumour and Reality." *Journal of Asian and African Studies* 14 (3–4): 191–203. http://dx.doi.org/10.1177/002190967901400301.

Agnew, Vijay. 1996. *Resisting Discrimination: Women from Asia, Africa and the Caribbean and the Women's Movement in Canada.* Toronto: University of Toronto Press.

– 2005. "Introduction." In *Diaspora, Memory, and Identity: A Search for Home,* ed. Vijay Agnew, 3–18. Toronto: University of Toronto Press.

– ed. 2007. *Interrogating Race and Racism.* Toronto: University of Toronto Press.

Ahmed, Leila. 2011. *A Quiet Revolution: The Veil Resurgence, from the Middle East to America.* New Haven: Yale University Press.

Anderson, Joan, and Sheryl Kirkham. 1998. "Constructing Nation: The Gendering and Racializing of the Canadian Health Care System." In *Painting the Maple: Essays on Race, Gender and the Construction of Canada,* ed. Veronica Strong-Boag, Sherill Grace, Avigali Eisenberg, and Joan Anderson, 242–61. Vancouver: UBC Press.

Anderson, Kay. 1991. *Vancouver's Chinatown: Racial Discourse in Canada, 1875–1980.* Montreal and Kingston: McGill-Queen's University Press.

Antz, P., and M. Lambek, eds. 1996. *Tense Past: Cultural Essays in Trauma and Memory.* New York: Routledge.

Armbruster, Heidi. 2008. "Introduction: The Ethics of Taking Sides." In *Taking Sides: The Ethics, Politics and Fieldwork in Anthropology,* ed. Heidi Armbruster and Anna Laerke, 1–22. New York: Berghahn.

Ayotte, Kevin J., and Mary E. Husain. 2005. "Securing Afghan Women: Neocolonialism, Epistemic Violence, and the Rhetoric of the Veil." *NWSA Journal* 17 (3): 112–33. http://dx.doi.org/10.2979/NWS.2005.17.3.112.

Azarbaijani-Moghaddam, Sippi. 2004. "Afghan Women on the Margins of the Twenty-First Century." In *Nation-Building Unraveled: Aid, Peace and Justice in Afghanistan,* ed. Antonio Donini, Norah Niland, and Karin Wermester, 95–116. Bloomfield, CT: Kumarian Press.

Baines, Gary. 2007. "The Master Narrative of South Africa's Liberation Struggle: Remembering and Forgetting June 16, 1976." *International Journal of African Historical Studies* 40 (2): 283–302.

Bairner, Alan. 2008. "The Cultural Politics of Remembrance: Sport, Place and Memory in Belfast and Berlin." *International Journal of Cultural Policy* 14 (4): 417–30. http://dx.doi.org/10.1080/10286630802445880.

Bannerji, Himani. 1995. *Thinking Through: Essays on Feminism, Marxism and Anti-racism.* Toronto: Women's Press.

– 2000. *The Darker Side of the Nation: Essays on Multiculturalism, Nationalism and Gender.* Toronto: Canadian Scholars' Press.

Barak, Oren. 2007. "Don't Mention the War? The Politics of Remembrance and Forgetfulness in Postwar Lebanon." *Middle East Journal* 61 (1): 49–70.

Barlow, Kathleen. 2004. "Critiquing the 'Good Enough' Mother: A Perspective Based on the Murik of Papua New Guinea." *Ethos* 32 (4): 514–37. http://dx.doi.org/10.1525/eth.2004.32.4.514.

Beverley, John. 1992. "The Margins at the Center: On Testimonio (Testimonial Narrative)." In *De/colonizing the Subject: The Politics of Gender in Women's Autobiography,* ed. Sidonie Smith and Julia Watson, 91–114. Minneapolis: University of Minnesota Press.

Bhatia, Prem Narain. 1973. *Indian Ordeal in Africa.* New Delhi: Vikas.

Boehm, Deborah A. 2012. *Intimate Migrations: Gender, Family and Illegality among Transnational Mexicans.* New York: New York University Press.

Bold, Christine, Ric Knowles, and Belinda Leach. 2002. "Feminist Memorializing and Cultural Countermemory: The Case of Marianne's Park." *Signs* 28 (1): 125–48. http://dx.doi.org/10.1086/340905.

Bourguignon, Erika. 2005. "Memory in an Amnesic World: Holocaust, Exile, and the Return of the Suppressed." *Anthropological Quarterly* 78 (1): 63–88. http://dx.doi.org/10.1353/anq.2005.0004.

Brand, Laurie A. 2010. "National Narratives and Migration: Discursive Strategies of Inclusion and Exclusion in Jordan and Lebanon." *International Migration Review* 44 (1): 78–110. http://dx.doi.org/10.1111/j.1747-7379.2009.00799.x.

Brodsky, Anne E. 2003. *With All Our Strength: The Revolutionary Association of the Women of Afghanistan.* New York: Routledge.

Butler, Judith. 2004. *Precarious Life: The Powers of Mourning and Violence.* New York: Verso.

– 2009. *Frames of War: When Is Life Grievable.* Brooklyn, NY: Verso.

Caesten, Janet. 1997. *The Heat of the Hearth: The Process of Kinship in a Malay Fishing Community.* New York: Oxford University Press.

Castillo, Rosalva Aída Hernández. 2012. "Cross-Border Mobility and Transnational Identities: New Border Crossings amongst Mexican Mam People." *Journal of Latin American and Caribbean Anthropology* 17 (1): 65–87. http://dx.doi.org/10.1111/j.1935-4940.2012.01190.x.

Chilton, Mariana, and Donald Rose. 2009. "A Rights-Based Approach to Food Insecurity in the United States." *American Journal of Public Health* 99 (7): 1203–11. http://dx.doi.org/10.2105/AJPH.2007.130229.

Collins, Patricia Hill. 2000. *Black Feminist Thought: Knowledge, Consciousness, and the Politics of Empowerment.* 2nd ed. New York: Routledge.

Cooley, John K. 1999. *Unholy Wars: Afghanistan, American and International Terrorism.* London: Pluto.

Crumley, Carole L. 2002. "Exploring Venus of Social Memory." In *Social Memory and History: Anthropological Perspectives*, ed. Jacob J. Climo and Maria G. Cattell, 39–52. New York: Bergin and Garvey.

Daniel, Valentine E. 1996. *Charred Lullabies: Chapters in an Anthropography of Violence.* Princeton: Princeton University Press.

Das, Veena. 1996. "Language and Body: Transactions in the Construction of Pain." *Daedalus* 125 (1): 67–91.

– 2003. "Trauma and Testimony: Implications for Political Community." *Anthropological Theory* 3 (3): 293–307. http://dx.doi.org/10.1177/14634996030033003.

– 2007. *Life and Words: Violence and the Descent into the Ordinary.* Berkeley: University of California Press.

Das, Veena, and Arthur Kleinman. 2001. "Introduction." In *Remaking a World: Violence, Social Suffering, and Recovery*, ed. Veena Das, Arthur Kleinman, Margaret Lock, Mamphela Ramphele, and Pamela Reynolds, 1–30. Berkeley: University of California Press. http://dx.doi.org/10.1525/california/9780520223295.003.0001.

Daulatzai, Anila. 2006. "Acknowledging Afghanistan: Notes and Queries on an Occupation." *Cultural Dynamics* 18 (3): 293–311. http://dx.doi.org/10.1177/0921374006071616.

– 2008. "The Discursive Occupation of Afghanistan." *British Journal of Middle East-ern Studies* 35 (3): 419–35. http://dx.doi.org/10.1080/13530190802532953.

Debouzy, Marianne. 1986. "In Search of Working-Class Memory: Some Ques-tions and a Tentative Assessment." *History and Anthropology* 2 (2): 261–82. http://dx.doi.org/10.1080/02757206.1986.9960769.

De Alwis, Malathi. 2001. "The 'Language of the Organs': The Political Purchase of Tears in Contemporary Shi Lanka." In *Haunting Violations: Feminist Criti-cism and the Crisis of the Real*, ed. S. Wendy Hesford and Wendy Kozol, 119–26. Chicago: University of Illinois Press.

– 2003. "Reflections on Gender and Ethnicity in Sri Lanka." In *Feminists under Fire: Exchanges across War Zones*, ed. Wenona Giles, Malathi de Alwis, Edith Klein, Neluka Silva, and Maja Korac. Toronto: Between the Lines

– 2004. "The 'Purity' of Displacement and the Reterritorialization of Longing: Muslim Women Refgees in North-Western Sri Lanka." In *Sites of Violence: Gender and Conflict Zones*, ed. Wenona Giles and Jennifer Hyndman, 213–31. California: University of California Press.

Degnen, Cathrine. 2005. "Relationality, Place, and Absence: A Three-Dimensional Perspective on Social Memory." *Sociological Review* 53 (4): 729–744. http://dx.doi.org/10.1111/j.1467-954X.2005.00593.x.

Donini, Antonio, Norah Niland, and Karin Wermester. 2004. *Nation-Building Unraveled: Aid, Peace and Justice in Afghanistan*. Bloomfield, CT: Kumarian Press.

Dossa, Parin. 1994. "Critical Anthropology and Life Stories: Case Study of Elderly Ismaili Canadians." *Journal of Cross-Cultural Gerontology* 9 (3): 335–54. http://dx.doi.org/10.1007/BF00978218.

– 2004. *Politics and Poetics of Migration: Narratives of Iranian Women from the Dias-pora*. Toronto: Canadian Scholars' Press.

– 2005. "'Witnessing' Social Suffering: Testimonial Narratives of Women from Afghanistan." *British Columbian Quarterly* 147: 27–49.

– 2009. *Racialized Bodies, Disabling Worlds: Storied Lives of Immigrant Muslim Women*. Toronto: University of Toronto Press.

Douglass, Ana, and Thomas A. Vogler, eds. 2003. *Witness and Memory: The Dis-course of Trauma*. New York: Routledge.

Dupree, Nancy Hatch. 1990. "A Socio-Cultural Dimension: Afghan Women Refugees in Pakistan." In *The Cultural Basis of Afghan Nationalism*, ed. Ewan W. Anderson and Nancy Hatch Dupree, 121–33. London: Print Publishers.

– 2004. "The Family during Crisis in Afghanistan." *Journal of Comparative Family Studies* 35 (2): 311–31.

Duruz, Jean. 2005. "Eating at the Borders: Culinary Journeys." *Environment and Planning, D: Society and Space* 23 (1): 51–69. http://dx.doi.org/10.1068/d52j.

Eisenstein, Zillah. 1996. *Hatreds: Racialized and Sexualized Conflicts in the 21st Century*. New York: Routledge.

Elyachar, Julia. 2005. *Markets of Dispossession: NGOs, Economic Development and the State of Cairo*. Durham, NC: Duke University Press. http://dx.doi. org/10.1215/9780822387138.

Fanon, Frantz. 1963. *The Wretched of the Earth*. Trans. Constance Farrington. New York: Grove.

Farmer, Paul. 2003. *Pathologies of Power: Health, Human Rights, and the New War on the Poor*. Berkeley: University of California Press. http://dx.doi.org/10.1525/ nad.2003.6.1.1.

Fassin, Didier. 2007. *When Bodies Remember: Experiences and Politics of AIDS in South Africa*. Berkeley: University of California Press. http://dx.doi.org/ 10.1525/california/9780520244672.001.0001.

Fassin, Didier, and Richard Rechtman. 2009. *The Empire of Trauma: An Inquiry into the Condition of Victimhood*. Trans. Rachael Gomme. Princeton, NJ: Princeton University Press.

Feldman, Allen. 1991. *Formations of Violence: The Narrative of the Body and Political Terror in Northern Ireland*. Chicago: University of Chicago Press. http://dx.doi. org/10.7208/chicago/9780226240800.001.0001.

– 1994. "On Cultural Anesthesia: From Desert Storm to Rodney King." *American Anthropologist* 21 (2): 404–18.

Felman, Shoshana. 1992. "Educating and Crisis, or the Vicissitudes of Teaching." In *Trauma: Explorations in Memory*, ed. Cathy Caruth, 3–12. Baltimore: Johns Hopkins University Press.

Felman, Shoshana, and Dori Laub. 1992. *Testimony: Crisis of Witnessing in Literature, Psychoanalysis and History*. New York: Routledge.

Frank, Arthur. 1995. *The Wounded Storyteller*. Chicago: University of Chicago Press. http://dx.doi.org/10.7208/chicago/9780226260037.001.0001.

Frank, Gelya. 2000. *Venus on Wheels: Two Decades of Dialogue on Disability, Biography, and Being Female in America*. Berkeley: University of California Press.

Frenz, Margret. 2013. "Migration, Identity and Post-Colonial Change in Uganda: A Goan Perspective." *Immigrants and Minorities* 31 (1): 48–73. http://dx.doi.org/10.1080/02619288.2012.746864.

Ghafour, Hamida. 2007. *Sleeping Buddha: The Story of Afghanistan through the Eyes of One Family*. London: Constable and Robinson.

Giles, Wenona, and Jennifer Hyndman, eds. 2004. *Sites of Violence: Gender and Conflict Zones*. Berkeley: University of California Press.

Giles, Wenona, Malathi de Alwis, Edith Klein, Neluka Silva, and Maja Korac, eds. 2003. *Feminists under Fire: Exchanges across War Zones*. Toronto: Between the Lines.

Ginsborg, Paul. 2005. *The Politics of Everyday Life: Making Choices Changing Lives.*
London: Yale University Press.

Goodson, Larry P. 2001. *Afghanistan's Endless War: State Failure, Regional Politics,
and the Rise of the Taliban.* Seattle: University of Washington Press.

Grima, Benedicte. 1992. *The Performance of Emotion among Paxtun Women: "The
Misfortunes which Have Befallen Me.* Austin: University of Texas Press.

Gvion, Liora. 2006. "Cuisines of Poverty as Means of Empowerment: Arab
Food in Israel." *Agriculture and Human Values* 23 (3): 299–312. http://dx.doi.
org/10.1007/s10460-006-9003-7.

Hastrup, Kirsten. 2003. "Violence, Suffering and Human Rights: Anthropological Reflections." *Anthropological Theory* 3 (3): 309–23. http://dx.doi.
org/10.1177/14634996030033004.

Hesford, Wendy, and Wendy Kozol, eds. 2001. *Haunting Violations: Feminist Criti-
cism and the Crisis of the Real.* Chicago: University of Illinois Press.

Hirschkind, Charles, and Saba Mahmood. 2002. "Feminism, the Taliban and
Politics of Counter-Insurgency." *Anthropological Quarterly* 75 (2): 339–54.
http://dx.doi.org/10.1353/anq.2002.0031.

Holtzman, Jon D. 2006. "Food and Memory." *Annual Review of Anthropology*
35 (1): 361–78. http://dx.doi.org/10.1146/annurev.anthro.35.081705.123220.

Hua, Ana. 2005. "Diaspora and Cultural Memory." In *Diaspora, Memory and
Identity: A Search for Home,* ed. Vijay Agnew, 191–208. Toronto: University of
Toronto Press.

Jackson, Michael. 2006. *The Politics of Storytelling: Violence, Transgression and Inter-
subjectivity.* Copenhagen: Museum Tusclanum Press.

Jiwani, Yasmin. 2006. *Discourses of Denial: Mediations of Race, Gender, and Violence.*
Vancouver: UBC Press.

Johnson, Chris, and Jolyon Leslie. 2002. "Afghans Have Their Memories: A Reflection on the Recent Experience of Assistance in Afghanistan." *Third World
Quarterly* 23 (5): 861–74. http://dx.doi.org/10.1080/0143659022000028611.

– 2004. *Afghanistan: The Mirage of Peace.* New York: Zed.

Joseph, Cynthia. 2013. "(Re)negotiating Cultural and Work Identities Pre- and
Post-migration: Malaysian Migrant Women in Australia." *Women's Studies International Forum* 36 (1): 27–36. http://dx.doi.org/10.1016/j.wsif.2012.10.002.

Kadar, Marlene. 2005. "Wounding Events and the Limits of Autobiography."
In *Diaspora, Memory and Identity: A Search for Home,* ed. Vijay Agnew, 81–109.
Toronto: University of Toronto Press.

Kandiyoti, Deniz. 2005. *The Politics of Gender and Reconstruction in Afghanistan.*
Occasional Paper 4. Geneva: United Nations Research Institute for Social
Development.

– 2007. "Old Dilemmas or New Challenges? The Politics of Gender and Reconstruction in Afghanistan." *Development and Change* 38 (2): 169–99. http://dx.doi.org/10.1111/j.1467-7660.2007.00408.x.

Kent, George. 2005. *Freedom from Want: The Human Right to Adequate Food.* Washington, DC: Georgetown University Press.

– 2010. "The Human Right to Food and Dignity." *Human Rights* 37 (1): 3–6.

– 2011. "Using the Right to Food to Teach Human Rights." In *Rights-Based Approaches to Public Health*, ed. Elvira Beracochea, Corey Weinstein, and Dabney Evans, 155–66. New York: Springer.

Khan, Shahnaz. 2001. "Between Here and There: Feminist Solidarity and Afghan Women." *Genders* 33. http://www.genders.org/g33/g33_kahn.html Accessed 20 Mar. 2008.

– 2008. "From Rescue to Recognition: Rethinking the Afghan Conflict." *Topia: Canadian Journal of Cultural Studies* 19: 115–36.

Khattak, Saba Gul. 2002. "Afghan Women: Bombed to Be Liberated." *Middle East Report* 222 (32): 18–23. http://dx.doi.org/10.2307/1559266.

Kim, Christine, Melina Baum Singer, and Sophie McCall. 2012. *Cultural Grammars of Nation, Diaspora and Indigeneity in Canada.* Waterloo: Wilfrid Laurier University Press.

Kirmayer, Laurence J. 2002. "The Refugee's Predicament." *L'Évolution Psychiatrique* 67 (4): 724–42. http://dx.doi.org/10.1016/S0014-3855(02)00166-4.

– 2003. "Failure of Imagination: The Refugee's Narrative in Psychiatry." *Anthropology and Medicine* 10 (2): 167–85. http://dx.doi.org/10.1080/13648470320 00122843.

Kirmayer, Laurence J., and Ellen Corin. 1998. "Inside Knowledge: Cultural Constructions of Insight in Psychosis." In *Insight and Psychosis*, ed. Xavier Francisco Amador and Anthony S. David, 193–220. New York: Oxford University Press.

Kleinman, Arthur, Veena Das, and Margaret M. Lock, eds. 1997. *Social Suffering.* Berkeley: University of California Press.

Kleinman, Arthur, and Joan Kleinman. 1997. "The Appeal of Experience; The Dismay of Images: Cultural Appropriation of Suffering in Our Times." In *Social Suffering*, ed. Arthur Kleinman, Veena Das, and Margaret Lock, 1–24. Berkerly: University of California Press.

LaCapra, Dominick. 1999. "Trauma, Absence, Loss." *Critical Inquiry* 25 (4): 696–727. http://dx.doi.org/10.1086/448943.

Lambek, Michael, and Paul Antz. 1996. "Introduction: Forecasting Memory." In *Tense Past: Cultural Essays in Trauma and Memory*, ed. Paul Antz and Michael Lambek, xi–xxxviii. New York: Routledge.

Lee, Christopher. 2012. "Asian Canadian Critical Practice as Commemoration." In *Cultural Grammars of Nation, Diaspora and Indigeneity in Canada*, ed. Christine Kim, Melina Baum Singer, and Sophie McCall, 119–34. Waterloo: Wilfrid Laurier University Press.

Li, Peter S. 2003. *Destination Canada: Immigration Debates and Issues.* Oxford: Oxford University Press.

Lind, David, and Elizabeth Barham. 2004. "The Social Life of the Tortilla: Food, Cultural Politics, and Contested Commodification." *Agriculture and Human Values* 21 (1): 47–60. http://dx.doi.org/10.1023/B:AHUM.0000014018. 76118.06.

Lindisfarne, Nancy. 2008. "Starting from Below: Fieldwork, Gender and Imperialism Now." In *Taking Sides: Ethics, Politics, and Fieldwork in Anthropology*, ed. Heidi Armbruster and Anna Laerke, 23–44. New York: Berghahn.

Lock, Margaret, and Patricia Kaufert. 1998. *Pragmatic Women and Body Politics.* Cambridge: Cambridge University Press.

Lopez, Mario. 2012. "Reconstituting the Affective Labour of Filipinos as Care Workers in Japan." *Global Networks* 12 (2): 252–68. http://dx.doi.org/ 10.1111/j.1471-0374.2012.00350.x.

Low, Setha M. 2011. "Claiming Space for an Engaged Anthropology: Spatial Inequality and Social Exclusion." *American Anthropologist* 113 (3): 389–407.

Lyons, Natasha. 2010. "The Wisdom of Elders: Inuvialuit Social Memories of Continuity and Change in the Twentieth Century." *Arctic Anthropology* 47 (1): 22–38. http://dx.doi.org/10.1353/arc.0.0034.

Malinowski, Bronislaw. 1922. *Malinowski and the Work of Myth.* Princeton: Princeton University Press.

Malkki, Liisa Helena. 1995. *Purity and Exile: Violence, Memory and National Cosmology among Hutu Refugees in Tanzania.* Chicago: University of Chicago Press.

– 1996. "Speechless Emissaries: Refugees, Humanitarianism, and Dehistoricization." *Cultural Anthropology* 11 (3): 377–404. http://dx.doi.org/10.1525/ can.1996.11.3.02a00050.

Mani, Lata. 1998. *Contentious Traditions: The Debate on Sati in Colonial India.* Berkerley: University of California Press.

Mankekar, Purnima. 2002. "India 'Shopping': Indian Grocery Stores and Transnational Configurations of Belonging." *Ethnos: Journal of Anthropology* 67 (1): 75–97. http://dx.doi.org/10.1080/00141840220122968.

Marchione, T.J., and E. Messer. 2010. "Food Aid and the World Hunger Solution: Why the U.S. Should use a Human Rights Approach." *Food and Foodways* 18 (1–2): 10–27. http://dx.doi.org/10.1080/07409711003708199.

Meintjes, Sheila, Anu Pillay, and Meredth Turshen. 2001. *The Aftermath: Women in Post-conflict Transformation.* London: Zed.

Morris, H. 1956 "Indians in East Africa." *British Journal of Sociology* 7 (1): 194-221

Mountz, Alison, and Richard A. Wright. 1996. "Daily Life in the Transnational Migrant Community of San Augustı'n, Oaxaca, and Poughkeepsie, New York." *Diaspora* 5 (3): 403–28. http://dx.doi.org/10.1353/dsp.1996.0017.

Moore, Henrietta L. 1988. *Feminism and Anthropology*. Minneapolis: University of Minnesota Press.

– ed. 1996. *The Future of Anthropological Knowledge*. London: Routledge.

– ed. 2000. *Anthropological Theory Today*. Malden, MA: Polity.

Moyo, Dambisa. 2009. *Dead Aid: Why Aid Is Not Working and How There Is Another Way for Africa*. London: Allen Lane.

Nagel, Caroline. 2005. "Introduction." In *Geographies of Muslim Women: Gender Religion, and Space*, ed. Ghazi-Walid Falah and Caoline Nagel, 1–18. New York: Guilford.

Ndebele, Njabulo S. 1994. *South African Literature and Culture: Rediscovery of the Ordinary*. Manchester: Manchester University Press.

Nordstrom, Carolyn. 2007. "War on the Front Lines." In *Ethnographic Fieldwork: An Anthropological Reader*, ed. Antonius C.G.M. Robben and Jeffrey A. Sluka, 245–58. Sidney: Blackwell.

Nordstrom, Carolyn, and Antonius C.G.M. Robben. 1995. *Fieldwork under Fire: Contemporary Studies of Violence and Survival*. Berkeley: University of California Press.

Ong, Aihwa. 1995. "Women Out of China: Traveling Tales and Traveling Theories in Postcolonial Feminism." In *Women Writing Culture*, ed. Ruth Behar and Deborah A. Gordon, 350–72. Berkeley: University of California Press.

Pasura, Dominic. 2013. "Modes of Incorporation and Transnational Zimbabwean Migration to Britain." *Ethnic and Racial Studies* 36 (1): 199–218. http://dx.doi.org/10.1080/01419870.2011.626056.

Phelps, Teresa Goodwin. 2004. *Shattered Voices: Language, Violence, and the Work of Truth Commissions*. Philadelphia: University of Pennsylvania Press.

Quesada, James, Laurie Kain Hart, and Philippe Bourgois. 2011. "Structural Vulnerability and Health: Latino Migrant Laborers in the United States." *Medical Anthropology* 30 (4): 339–62. http://dx.doi.org/10.1080/01459740.2011.576725.

Radin, Margaret Jane. 1996. *Contested Commodities*. Cambridge, MA: Harvard University Press.

Ray, Krishnendu. 2004. *The Migrant's Table: Meals and Memories in Bengali-American Households*. Philadelphia: Temple University Press.

Razack, Sherene H. 1998. *Looking White People in the Eye: Gender, Race, and Culture in Courtrooms and Classrooms*. Toronto: University of Toronto Press.

– 2000. "From the 'Clean Snows of Petawawa': The Violence of Canadian Peace-keepers in Somalia." *Cultural Anthropology* 15 (1): 127–63. http://dx.doi.org/10.1525/can.2000.15.1.127.

– 2002. "Gendered Racial Violence and Spatialized Justice: The Murder of Pamela George." In *Race, Space, and the Law: Unmapping a White Settler Society*, ed. Sherene H. Razack, 121–57. Toronto: Between the Lines.

Razack, Sherene, Malinda Smith, and Sunera Thobani, eds. 2010. *States of Race: Critical Race Feminism for the 21st Century*. Toronto: Between the Lines.

Rosenberger, Nancy. 2007. "Patriotic Appetites and Gnawing Hungers: Food and the Paradox of Nation-Building in Uzebekistan." *Ethos* 72 (3): 339–60.

Ross, Fiona C. 2001. "Speech and Silence: Women's Testimony in the First Five Weeks of Public Hearings of the South African Truth and Reconciliation Commission." In *Remaking a World: Violence, Social Suffering and Recovery*, ed. Veena Das, Aurthur Kleinman, Margaret Lock, Mamphela Ramphele, and Pamela Reynolds, 225–80. Berkeley: University of California Press.

– 2003. *Bearing Witness: Women and the Truth and Reconciliation Commission in South Africa*. London: Pluto.

Rubin, Barnett R. 1995. *The Search for Peace in Afghanistan: From Buffer State to Failed State*. New Haven: Yale University Press.

– 2000. "The Political Economy of War and Peace in Afghanistan." *World Development* 28 (10): 1789–1803. http://dx.doi.org/10.1016/S0305-750X(00)00054-1.

– 2002. *The Fragmentation of Afghanistan: State Formation and Collapse in the International System*. 2nd ed. New Haven: Yale University Press.

Said, Edward. 1978. *Orientalism*. New York: Vintage.

Saikal, Amin. 2006. *Modern Afghanistan: A History of Struggle and Survival*. London: I.B. Tauris.

Salari, Sonia. 2002. "Invisible in Aging Research: Arab Americans, Middle Eastern Immigrants, and Muslims in the United States." *Gerontologist* 42 (5): 580–8. http://dx.doi.org/10.1093/geront/42.5.580.

Scheper-Hughes, Nancy. 1992. *Death without Weeping: The Violence of Everyday Life in Brazil*. Berkeley: University of California Press.

Scheper-Hughes, Nancy, and Philippe Bourgois. 2004. *Violence in War and Peace: An Anthology*. Malden, MA: Blackwell.

Shahrani, Nazif M. 2002. "War, Factionalism, and the State in Afghanistan." *American Anthropologist* 104 (3): 715–22. http://dx.doi.org/10.1525/aa.2002.104.3.715.

Silove, D., Z. Steel, and C. Watters. 2000. "Policies of Deterrence and the Mental Health of Asylum Seekers." *Journal of the American Medical Association* 284 (5): 604–11. http://dx.doi.org/10.1001/jama.284.5.604.

Smith, Dorothy E. 1987. *The Everyday World as Problematic: A Feminist Sociology*. Boston: Northeastern University Press.

– 1999. *Writing the Social: Critique, Theory, and Investigations*. Toronto: University of Toronto Press.

Smith, Joe, and Petr Jehlicka. 2007. "Stories around Food, Politics and Change in Poland and the Czech Republic." *Transactions of the Institute of British Geographers* 32 (3): 395–410. http://dx.doi.org/10.1111/j.1475-5661.2007.00258.x.

Soto, Lilia. 2012. "On Becoming Mexican in Napa: Mexican Immigrant Girls Negotiating Challenges to Transnational Identities." *Social Identities* 18 (1): 19–37. http://dx.doi.org/10.1080/13504630.2012.629509.

Spitzer, Denise L. 2011. *Engendering Migrant Health: Canadian Perspectives*. Toronto: University of Toronto Press.

Stabile, Carol A., and Deepa Kumar. 2005. "Unveiling Imperialism: Media, Gender and the War on Afghanistan." *Media, Culture and Society* 27 (5): 765–82. http://dx.doi.org/10.1177/0163443705055734.

Stockton, Nicholas. 2004. "Afghanistan, War, Aid and International Order." In *Nation-Building Unraveled: Aid, Peace and Justice in Afghanistan*, ed. Antonio Donini, Norah Niland, and Karin Wermester, 9–38. Bloomfield, CT: Kumarian Press.

Sugiman, Pamela. 2004. "Memories of Internment: Narrating Japanese Canadian Women's Life Stories." *Canadian Journal of Sociology* 29 (3): 359–88. http://dx.doi.org/10.2307/3654672.

– 2009. "'Life Is Sweet': Vulnerability and Composure in the Wartime Narratives of Japanese Canadians." *Journal of Canadian Studies / Revue d'études canadiennes* 43 (1): 186–218.

Thobani, Sunera. 2003. "War and the Politics of Truth-Making in Canada." *Qualitative Studies in Education* 16 (3): 399–414. http://dx.doi.org/10.1080/0951839032000086754.

– 2007. *Exalted Subjects: Studies in the Making of Race and Nation in Canada*. Toronto: University of Toronto Press.

– 2011. "Introduction." In *Race, Immigration, and the Canadian State*. SA345–4 Study Guide, 7–11. Centre for Online and Distance Education. Burnaby: Simon Fraser University.

Todeschini, Maya. 2001. "The Bomb's Womb? Women and the Atom Bomb." In *Remaking a World: Violence, Social Suffering, and Recovery*, ed. Veena Das, Arthur Kleinman, Margaret Lock, Mamphela Ramphele, and Pamela Reynolds, 102–56. Berkeley: University of California Press.

Turton, David, and Peter Marsden. 2002. *Taking Refugees for a Ride? The Politics of Refugee Return to Afghanistan*. Kabul: Afghanistan Research and Evaluation Unit.

Walks, Michelle, and Naomi McPherson, eds. 2011. *An Anthropology of Mothering*. Toronto: Demeter.

Waterson, Roxana. 2007. "Trajectories of Memory: Documentary Film and the Transmission Testimony." *History and Anthropology* 18 (1): 51–73. http://dx.doi.org/10.1080/02757200701218239.

Werbner, Richard. 1998. "Smoke from the Barrel of a Gun: Postwars of the Dead, Memory and Reinscription in Zimbabwe." In *Memory and the Postcolony: African Anthropology and the Critique of Power*, ed. Richard P. Werbner, 71–102. London: Zed.

Zarowsky, Christina. 2004. "Writing Trauma: Emotion, Ethnography, and the Politics of Suffering among Somali Refugees in Ethiopia." *Culture, Medicine and Psychiatry* 28 (2): 189–209. http://dx.doi.org/10.1023/B:MEDI.0000034410.08428.29.

Index

Page numbers in italics refer to photographs.